A HOME FORUM READER

A HOME FORUM READER

A timeless collection of essays and poems
from the Home Forum Page
of The Christian Science Monitor®

COMPILED and EDITED
by
FREDERIC HUNTER

Books from

THE CHRISTIAN SCIENCE MONITOR.

Boston, Massachusetts

The essays and poems in this book were originally published in *The Christian Science Monitor.*

This book was designed by Yellow Inc., Needham, Massachusetts. It was typeset in Sabon by C W Graphics, Inc., Holbrook, Massachusetts. Jackets produced by New England Book Components, Inc., Hingham, Massachusetts. It was printed and bound in the U.S.A. by Semline Book Group, Braintree, Massachusetts.

ISBN 0-87510-196-8

A Home Forum Reader
Introduction

Journalism around the world offers few examples of sections unique to one newspaper. The Christian Science Monitor's Home Forum is such an exception. Unique to the Monitor, the Home Forum seeks to answer the Monitor's special charge not merely to publish facts and trends and analyses of them, but also to provide readers with material of lasting interest.

For eight decades the Home Forum has offered this special kind of material. The Home Forum publishes it in a volume and with a regularity found in no other daily publication. In recent years the Home Forum has concentrated on personal essays, some very funny, and cultural musings; commentaries on the arts with an occasional interview with an artist; and short poetry which is both accessible to a wide audience and suitable to a family readership. Although essays comprise the bulk of this volume, it also includes a selection of sonnets by Home Forum poets.

The Home Forum is also unusual in that it welcomes contributions from virtually any writer who wishes to submit. This means that its editors review submissions from a broad spectrum of writers, from established authors like Doris Peel and David Mazel to a writer like Jim Comstock whom they have published only once. Home Forum editors read every manuscript submitted. They circulate those with potential among the staff. Although much material proves unsuitable, the general level of the submissions strikes the editors as remarkably high. This affords them the occasional delight of discovering a small gem—like Thomas Palakeel's "Dreams of Elephants" which arrived in the mail one day from Grand Forks, North Dakota.

In assembling this anthology we decided that, with so many contributors to choose from, no writer should be represented by more than one essay. We confirm rules by making exceptions to them. Here we have included three pieces by Alex Noble because hers are extremely brief. We have selected three essays by the husband-and-wife writing team of Jan and Harry Lee

Little; as a unit their essays record one chapter in a noteworthy pioneering adventure which Home Forum readers followed for many years.

The essays in this reader were written over a period of three decades. While dealing with matters of lasting interest, the essays also reflect their times. Several from the late '60s and early '70s, for example, deal with efforts of writers—and by extension, presumably, the society at large—to discuss new ways of thinking, new ways of behaving, at a time of turmoil and change. An appendix lists the dates of original publication of the various pieces and, in those cases where they have been altered, their original titles.

Mary Baker Eddy, the Monitor's founder, envisioned the paper as blessing all mankind. Like the Home Forum itself, these essays and sonnets offer readers the world, both in a geographical sense and in the sense of the world of the heart. We hope that they bless you in the few hours you give to reading them. 🐗

Frederic Hunter

CONTENTS

THE
LIVELY ARTS

SILENCE
David Holmstrom

The cabin was a gift. A voice over the telephone said, "Of course it's the perfect place to write your book. ❧ There are no houses within ten miles and the desert is beautifully quiet. ❧ It's a large cabin and there is a refrigerator, and a stove, not to mention a large fireplace and the wood stacked outside waiting. ❧ Consider it your home for as long as you like. The key is under the third stone from the faucet." ❧

Before the week was out he was there, surrounded by an immense brown desert floor that stretched out over one hundred miles to the Tehachapis on the far horizon and curled upward behind the cabin through the low and dusty trees to the sides of the San Gabriel mountains towering in the south.

The cabin was not the kind of cabin that leaps to the mind's eye when one thinks of an isolated cabin. It was made of cement blocks and had a wide screened-in front porch, a smiling pot-bellied stove to complement the fireplace ("snow in two months," the voice over the telephone had warned), a closet-sized kitchen, old, comfortable furniture, many windows and the crisp smell of clear air.

He settled down quickly and arranged the few things he had brought along—favorite books, a stack of paper, plenty of food—and then, like a whisper, just as he began to write, he discovered the problem of the ages: silence. Not the silence of daylight hours when the blank was gently filled with wind in the trees or wind through the screens or an occasional bird; it was the complete and photographic stillness of those first few nights when nothing moved or turned.

"You cannot imagine the silence here," he wrote to a friend. "It is absolute, not a sound. It awes me to the bone. Last night I took my flashlight and walked to a promontory that juts out like a throne above the desert. The stars were embedded in the blackness with such precision and joy that I felt an audience was watching me. I sat for an hour. All thoughts of noise, of cities, of the unavoidable buzz of daily life where you are reading this, left me. Before too long a soft moon eased its way around the earth and hung like a plate twenty feet above the horizon. I could not move.

"In the silence I began to hear a muffled flapping sound coming somewhere from my left. I listened, barely hearing it. It came closer, louder. I squinted in the darkness for some sort of movement. Then, overhead, I saw it. A large bird was making its way across the sky. Its huge wings brushed the night air in a steady sound of thrust and recovery. The lone sound in all the world was the effort of his wings. In a few seconds I saw the bird pass in front of the moon like a hand and disappear. I have never before heard the sound of a bird flying."

Within two weeks, and with considerable effort, the writer grew comfortably into the silence. He discovered he could find very small sounds coming from great distances either from memory or actuality. In the early morning hours when the sun had not yet shown itself but covered the desert with a vague, glowing orange, and he had stayed awake all night writing and rewriting—in those early hours he could now hear the waking sounds he had missed before. A hidden animal scratching, a leaf falling ("Yes," he wrote, "a leaf striking the earth makes a definite and pleasing crunch."), and the hum of a truck thirty miles away.

A month passed and he reckoned himself to be in control. The writing was flowing; his characters argued about themselves, moved throughout the cabin and settled down on paper. All was well until the first snow fell.

"I switched off the light and sat by the window in the darkness that night. Outside the fresh snow was a foot deep. Covering the ground it was nearly translucent, as if deep within the shell of the earth a light shone. I leaned back and, as had become my habit, I listened intently for any new sounds which hid themselves in the heart of silence. What I heard was a nearly imperceptible mixture of scraping and parting as if a small foot was pushing its way cautiously into the snow.

"I saw the deer just then. He came toward the window, testing each foothold with infinite patience before he took another step. Six feet away he stopped and nibbled at the greenery on a tree. While he chewed he seemed to stare at me, although I am sure he did not suspect that in the darkness a

2

man sat so near. I could hear him chewing. It was a rumbling, grating sound like dough being kneaded. His neck was trim and strong. Had it not been for the reflected whiteness of the snow the animal would have blended into the night. Was he watching me? Were his eyes seeing me or nothing?

"When my chair squeaked loudly, so loudly that it shattered the stillness and seemed like a bomb, the animal's first and instant bound away from the cabin was at least eight feet in length. He simply exploded away with such speed and power that he was there and then he was not. For a few seconds I heard him crashing through the underbrush and then fade to nothing."

It was at this chronological point that the writer began to, as he put it, "percolate with dissatisfaction over the role of fiction." The question arose in his thought, like a bounding deer, that perhaps, just perhaps, fiction, for all its triumphs and endurance, was taking the long way around to say something essentially non-fictional.

In writing to a friend the writer mocked himself: "I saw and heard a wild deer last night. He was less than six feet away from me, standing in the snow. This experience has left me limp. There are no words (I cannot find any at all) to describe the mystery of silence that enveloped us as we faced each other. It cannot be translated to the measurement of words. And yet I am bursting to tell of it. But I cannot. There remains a silence, an area of reality which forbids accurate reporting of what occurred. I am stunned to think that perhaps by default—a failure to tell what is real—fiction preened its way into the world simply to make a little noise."

He continued his writing, now more like discharging a pleasant duty than recording the vitality of mythical people facing problems within the confines of a beginning, middle and end. But the question continued to hang over him in the silence. In the whole range of human action and reaction, is there an unseen and unspeakable core out of reach to a fictional tone?

More than ever now he placed himself before the crackling fireplace with the lights out. He discovered that besides the strong urge to write a long story—an urge which had always been with him—he was now dividing his days between writing his long story, and writing about discovering silence. Neither was like the other. One had form, the other searched for form; and yet increasingly they began to depend on one another, to welcome each other's

3

contrast the way a child plays hard all Saturday and sleeps soundly all night.

In the last month he thought he noticed improvement, not so much in the process of writing, for that is not dependent on any known model, but improvement in what the writing was leading to. He used fewer adjectives, fewer adverbs; his paragraphs were lean and simple. His characters began to "express a little more humor in their plight" he wrote later.

"I suppose the change, if it must be called something, came upon me because I discovered the voice of silence. It is so uncomplicated to sit quietly and listen. While it takes a little practice to do it easily, it does help to have a great and silent land around you which eventually compels you to sit quietly and listen."

In four months he finished his book. "I am reluctant to leave," he wrote just before he left the cabin. "Yet I have accomplished what I set out to do. The bonus I discovered along the way is permanent. The book, I feel, might have its day. But it seems to me it will eventually give way to silence." 🐾

POTTING AND POETRY
Paul O. Williams

Recently I took a course in potting. ❧ I learned some things about throwing pots, and sometimes they threw me. ❧ But among the sagging rims and potbellied clay blobs, I learned something else that was pure serendipity. ❧ As a longtime poet and novice potter, I saw alliances and analogies between the two endeavors that truly surprised me. ❧

For instance, there is a certain cooperation between the material and the artist that is fascinating to watch. The clay at times seems to yearn to be a pot, the words to shape themselves into a poem. Both clay and phrases tend to determine by their nature what results are possible. The walls of the pot rise between the guiding hands of the potter, and if he or she is experienced, they do the potter's bidding with a remarkable sense of harmony.

But one can't make square pots on a wheel, nor can one violate the nature and limits of words and make a poem. Words mean only certain things, and send out only certain implications. One has to work with them, not against them—with their sounds, meanings, radiations, and the way they mesh with other words. But when the poem is spilling out, often all the melding happens effortlessly, as though the words found one another in an eager desire to become a poem.

Similarly, one discovers that much of the virtue of the pot lies in the properties of the materials themselves. This seems especially true when one gets to glazing. What one envisions beforehand is not precisely what one gets, and the results can surprise with their beauty.

The same is true with words, phrases, sounds, rhythms, images, meta-

5

phors. In fact, until this analogy became clear to me, I had never fully seen what natural virtue the materials of poems have, and how with such extraordinary materials, the poems that arise from our uses of them have a remarkable amount of help to give, of resources to pour out on the poet. Some words emit auras that seem romantic or fascinating. How could a "tundra" be other than bleak, a "blimp" other than rounded? An "eolith," or "dawn stone," carries the romance of the very ancient in its being and sound. Does not "Chattanooga" invite a song with rhythm, or "Walla Walla" sound faintly risible? Putting together images, the poet creates metaphors that bear a sense of meaning never seen before, as when Sylvia Plath says of a newborn child's cry, "The clear vowels rise like balloons." Her contribution to the result is perhaps less than that of the resources ready for her hand, precise as her comparison is.

The wealth of sounds is also there for the poet's use. When Frost began his poem, "Tree at my window, window tree," he set a music going in his readers through the repetition and variation of the particular sounds he used. We have a feel about the poem before we are well into it—and this is possible because of the virtue of the sounds and rhythms themselves. Repeating the phrase in inversion not only gives us the double meaning of identifying the tree and describing it as a place of symbolic insight. It also juxtaposes sounds, bright and dark, stopped and drawn out. While the poet uses these skillfully, still they were awaiting his use, and his poem is made from what was ready for him.

Of course there are limits. In potting, if one asks the clay to do things it is incapable of doing, it revenges itself by collapsing. In poetry, one cannot transgress what words are capable of, nor can poets ever really assure themselves that their meanings are either lucid to everyone or as evocative as they would like them to be.

Roger, my ceramics instructor, remarked when I explained that I had accomplished something by doing it in a way I wasn't supposed to: "You can't cheat." If it works, you haven't. If you try something that doesn't work, you obviously don't get away with it. In poetry, if your rime words dominate their lines, you have tried to complete a poem without real care or effort. The result collapses like a top-heavy pot.

Machines can make ceramic pieces more regularly than the human hand. But as a sign in the studio reads, "A perfectly centered pot is a dead pot." The subtle variations that give ceramic pieces their individuality also give them interest and bring us delight. So, too, a perfectly regular poem in traditional form is generally a dull one, and the interplay between expectations and actualities imparts beauty and meaning to the result. For example, Poe, who is not known for metrical irregularities, opens his poem "To Helen" with the following stanza:

> *Helen, thy beauty is to me*
> *Like those Nicean barks of yore*
> *That gently, o'er a perfumed sea,*
> *The weary, way-worn wanderer bore*
> *To his own native shore.*

Basically iambic, the meter is varied by an inverted first foot and significant departures in the fourth line, including a spondee and an extra unaccented syllable. In addition, the pauses in Lines 3 and 4, themselves of different length, impart variety and interest to the stanza. Yet we recognize it as basically regular.

Like pots, poems sometimes absolutely demand to be left alone, even when the poet would like to continue polishing them. Pots of much beauty will collapse under such improvements. So do poems. Both seem to delight in their own individualities.

Up to a point, that is. My own best potting effort, a green jar with a lid, sits on my mantel, leaning very slightly. I have turned it so the viewer can see the lean. It seems only honest. Still, I wonder. I have written some poems that lean, and in which the angularity seemed a virtue. But I knew I was doing it. As to the pot, I am less sure. I think I imparted the lean to it in separating it from the wheel. It seems faintly amusing. Roger raised an eyebrow at it—only slightly, as is his habit. I think he meant I was more of a poet than a potter. That is no doubt true. My final notion is that poems, like pots, should not lean by mistake but by intent or serendipity. 🐌

A MUSICAL EDUCATION IN SHANGHAI
Enid Saunders Candlin

M y White Russian music teacher, Mr. Leibensohn, had come to Shanghai as a refugee, but continued to feel himself a native of Petrograd, as he persisted in calling it—Shanghai never had any real existence for him. 🐘 He had a great gift of teaching, and a delicate and lingering touch: It was he who introduced me to the music of John Field, and through him I came to feel close to that fugitive Irish genius who had so captured the admiration and affection of the Russians, and whose nocturnes are still identified with the long white nights, the magic silences, of that far-northern city. 🐘

Mr. Leibensohn was about five feet tall, and looked in every way like a leprechaun. It seemed incredible that so insubstantial, impractical, and dreamy a creature could ever have made his way through a conservatory, become a recognized teacher, married, survived the Revolution, trekked out of Russia and across Siberia, and then found his way down the China Coast as far as Shanghai—and yet here he was, even managing to exist reasonably well on his precarious profession. Much of this achievement was due to his wife, who seemed always to be preparing borsch or boeuf Stroganoff when I came for my lessons. Among the 7,000 White Russians who had fetched up in Shanghai they were perhaps the most touching, which was saying a great deal.

After 1917 the White Russians with money, influential friends, or a more cosmopolitan education had generally fled to Europe. It was the less fortunate who had struggled out via Siberia to China—and they could hardly have found a more difficult place to settle since the Chinese could do almost everything better and cheaper than anyone else, and the Western communities were all tied to their home countries. These bewildered, stateless newcomers were unprepared in practically every way for what lay ahead. They could at least stay—no one needed a passport to enter Shanghai.

And there were a few things the Chinese could not do better than these pitiful wanderers: One of them was to teach Western music. Here was a great city, the most cosmopolitan in the world, a Philistine place if ever there was one, but there was money in it, and among its transient, worldly populace many were genuinely fond of music. There were not enough Polish, German, Czech, Italian players on the Coast to supply this longing, and the musicians among the White Russians quickly realized this, found little rooms, rented uprights (all of which had been brought from the West), and set out to find pupils. These artists became a boon to us all—they made Shanghai less wholly materialistic.

The city came to have the only Western orchestra on the China Coast, with an Italian conductor and leader—Maestro Paci and Mr. Foa (whose sartorial elegance and wasp waist gave great pleasure to his public), and about eighty players, most of whom where White Russians. In time four Greek Orthodox churches were built by these indomitable people; many of us went to them at Easter and Christmas to hear their splendid choirs. And when singing competitions took place between the local schools it was found that the little White Russians put all their contemporaries to shame, with their beautiful voices, their fire, their intense musicality. They sang even better than the German children, till then by far the best in the field.

Every Christmas the Western schools gathered in the big, drafty, old Town Hall to sing their national songs. The English youngsters from the cathedral schools, in uniforms and blazers, worked dutifully through "The Holly and the Ivy," the Americans from the mission school rendered "Old Black Joe" in a style which even their doting parents felt was deplorable, the Lycée pupils trilled out some French airs, the Kaiser Wilhelm Schule contingent sang Lieder, almost professionally. Last of all, the shabby, stout Russian children rushed up to the platform, the poorest and youngest of all the groups. They were always so eager that they could hardly wait to begin, but they were highly disciplined, never taking their bright and shining eyes off the conductor's baton.   At his nod they burst into part singing and invariably brought down the house. We could never hear them enough, there or at the recitals the music teachers gave. On these occasions many of the performers would be so small that they had to be lifted up to the piano stool, where, waiting with rapt joy, they would poise their chubby hands high over the keys till the teacher gave them the signal to start, when they would swoop, forte, prestissimo, into great opening chords. With all this Slavic brilliance about a certain despair descended upon the rest of us.

But these same teachers encouraged us to press on, and no one was more gently persuasive than Mr. Leibensohn. Soon after I had come to him he gave me my first Field Nocturne—the Fifth—in a worn Polish edition with large brownish leaves. I fell in love with it at once. He spoke to me so often of Field, repeating old Petrograd stories, that I came to identify my leprechaun professor with the composer himself—they seemed in my imagination to partake of the same delicacy, the same dreaming quality, total devotion to music and an indifference to the world.

John Field was born in Dublin in 1782 of a family of musicians. Before he was ten he had made a successful debut there, and, soon after, another in London. He was then apprenticed to Clementi, who gave him lessons in exchange for his work in the Clementi piano shop, where the boy played on the pianos so exquisitely that people could not resist buying them. In 1802 Clementi took his pupil to Paris, where his playing and the few sonatas he published created a sensation: Then they went on to Germany and Russia. Spohr has left an account of the immense effect this pale, overgrown youth, wretchedly clothed, his sleeves almost up to his elbows, made on the Russians—the comparison between his magical, sensitive playing and the destitute condition to which Clementi's avarice had reduced him. They persuaded him to stay on in Russia and make it his home.

Field became the darling of the Russians, first in Petrograd, then in Moscow. He proved to be a remarkable teacher and students thronged to him: He wrote those nocturnes which are the forerunners of Chopin's and a

10

few other pieces, but he was careless and indifferent as to their publication or their collection. His deliberate movements, his silences, his reveries, the enchantment of his playing, became a legend. Liszt says: "Er bezauberte sein Publicum, ohne es zu wissen und ohne es zu wollen." (He bewitched his public, without knowing that he had, or wanting to.) We find him spoken of in the pages of "War and Peace," where Countess Rostova asks someone to play her one of the nocturnes. These idylls have a special grace about them, an elegance, at once sensitive and tender, apart from the world.

As I used to play them to Mr. Leibensohn, so long afterward, in that hybrid city on the China Coast, he would say often, "As you dream . . . as you dream . . . ," and caution me about the pedal capturing a chord only after it had been played—I must think of the ice forming on the shores of the Neva and the Bay, and sense the long summer twilights. I did, I still do, and I love Field for all this. I don't know what happened to Mr. Leibensohn; he was caught up like all the rest of us in the convulsions which overtook Shanghai, and we lost each other in the many years of war and their aftermath. But Field and his nocturnes remain. ❧

ART TO STUMBLE OVER
Christopher Andreae

There he is at the front door again, the Kleeneze Man, with his "shining morning face." ✿ It wears, as usual, a rosy smile which aptly mirrors his wares. ✿ His company hawks things like "new tools for flawless floors" and "everything for washday." ✿

He's visited us quite a few times before. But only this time do I find out that he's an Art Lover. Up to a point, anyway.

"I like your sculpture," he says.

The Andreae Collection does, in fact, include one or two modest sculptures, but they are indoors.

"Sculpture . . . ?"

He looks back over his shoulder, toward the gate.

"Ah," I laugh, "you mean the pebbles?"

"Yes, the piles of pebbles! V-e-r-y beautiful!" I suspect him of teasing me. "Mind you, they're much better than The Bricks I saw in the Gallery of Modern Art!" Yes, he's teasing.

I should explain. About both the bricks and the pebbles (or The Pebble Predicament, as it is known round here.)

First, The Bricks.

The Bricks are something of a *cause célèbre* in Britain. They have come to symbolize, in the eyes of almost everyone, the derisory absurdity, the expensive pointlessness, of "modern art." They belong to the Tate Gallery in London. The gallery bought them—and they were not cheap, and it was public money—some years ago when "minimal art" was considered a vital force in the art world.

The Bricks are the work of American sculptor Carl Andre—though it is the lack of evident *work* that constitutes one of the piece's main affronts to the general sensibility: Surely a "work of art" should not just claim to be art, it should also show quite clearly how much "work" the artist has put into it.

So The Bricks very soon became infamous. A TV personality named Fyfe Robertson, who had a rich Scottish accent and a down-to-earth way of latching on to popular issues, stood on camera beside The Bricks and, nationwide, gave them the benefit of his ironical, indignant mockery. Whatever else Carl Andre had or had not achieved with his bricks, he had succeeded beyond the dreams of most artists in gaining public attention. Robertson had served him brilliantly . . . .

The Bricks have joined Picasso in the majority British imagination as self-evident proof that modern art is rubbish. A snobbish or intellectual joke. A con.

Now this puts people like me in a somewhat awkward situation. I am a modern art buff. I think of Picasso as a quite astonishing giant of an artist. I actually like The Bricks. I firmly believe that anything that can engage the imagination, can stir or alter our vision of the surrounding world, can stamp its after-image on your mind, or can, above all, make you want to paint or sculpt or even pile bricks, is art and not trickery. A blank, stuffy, unresponding suspicion of it simply deprives people of all kinds of new experiences. An open mind does not make a fool of you—what, after all, have you got to lose?

But even so, I find it almost impossible not to laugh along with Fyfe and the Kleeneze man when they pour scorn on The Bricks and/or Picasso. There *is* something inherently daft about a national museum spending a ton of money for a neat rectangle of unassuming bricks.

There is something obviously eccentric about painting both eyes in a face on the same side of the nose. So what is the point of even trying to persuade these chuckling philistines that there are good reasons, even profound reasons, for such peculiar manifestations of the "art spirit"?

So-called "minimal art" was and is a special test for disbelievers. A row of metal boxes on the floor, or a bright red, smooth, and featureless plank propped against the wall, seemed on the face of it to be negative objects deprived of virtually all art interest. There was no complexity, no composition, no intriguing asymmetry, no balancing act, and no apparent human touch. Piling or stacking or ordering became sculptural methods instead of carving, modeling, constructing, or joining. There was a lot less sweat and a good deal more thought.

I haven't really given the Minimalists much attention lately. But the

13

Kleeneze man set me going again. It seems that Minimalism continues to make an impact on his imagination.

I have on my shelves a book called "Minimal Art, A Critical Anthology" published 20 years ago. In it is an article about Andre's bricks by David Bourdon. Two things in this essay particularly intrigue me. One is an explanation from Andre himself:

"My work," he said, "is atheistic, materialistic, and communistic. It's atheistic because it's without transcendent form, without spiritual or intellectual quality. Materialistic because it's made out of its own materials without pretension to other materials. And communistic because the form is equally accessible to all men." I happen to think that there's a fair bit of wordplay going on here, though I can see what he means.

The author Bourdon, however, wrote that the "deployment" of Andre's bricks "suggested an orderly Japanese rock garden, conducive to contemplation. Andre had wanted to drive the spectator back to his own sensibility . . ." —an assessment which, if true, denies any conventional understanding of the three words the artist himself chose to describe his work. Which brings me to the pebbles.

The thing is, there's something wonderfully enticing about pebbles. I find it impossible to stroll along a beach, for instance, without concentrating like a child on the pebbles. It's a search. The perfect pebble (and I hope that I'll never actually find it) is the result of a peculiarly harmonious agreement between it and the ocean, a conversation. "Mmm, just rub me a little more on this side, please," the pebble murmurs. "Ah, more . . . yes, more . . . roar, roar . . . more, more," answers the big-hearted sea (an exchange that takes a century or so, you understand).

The chosen few pebbles may find their way onto a windowsill or dressing table; a home is not a home without several pebbles artfully positioned.

The consummate example of this in my experience is the home (now museum) of J.S. Ede in Cambridge (England), called Kettle's Yard. The Edes not only welcomed you but showed you all their treasures—paintings by Christopher Wood and Ben Nicholson, sculpture by Gaudier-Brzeska . . . and pebbles. Pebbles arranged on tables in spiral patterns, uncoiling like a watch spring, getting progressively smaller, pebbles of lovely smoothness, there for no other reason than their natural beauty. In their own unassuming way they upstaged the other art.

It strikes me that these pebbles are really what came later to be called

14

"minimal art." But here they were not weightily underpinned with aesthetic theory. What sculptor has even approached a re-creation, an appreciation in his art, of the consummate simplicity of a fine pebble?

The extraordinary thing, of course, is that there is *one* sculptor who did just that—the Romanian-born Constantin Brancusi. In "The Newborn," carved out of white marble, Brancusi dared an unpretentiousness of form as childlike as a pebble. He went even further with his "Beginning of the World." The audacity of reducing sculpture to such simplicity is astonishing, the skill to achieve it far more remarkable. Only the ocean and the pebble, talking to each other, have ever managed it without thinking.

And that may partly explain why I have three enormous piles of pebbles on the sidewalk by our front gate. They are splendid pebbles, gathered from the northern Scottish beach at Lossiemouth. They have spent half this year decorating a pond in the Glasgow Garden Festival. When the Festival ended, I asked if I could buy some of them. I wanted only a few bags to put along the edge of the duck-pond and around a Chinese pot by the back door. But it had to be a truckload or nothing the supplier said. Being a pebble buff, I ordered a truckload. Twelve tons arrived one morning. It *was* rather more than I had anticipated. Clearly I have to be more ambitious with my duck-pond.

But perhaps, after all, the Kleeneze man is right. They're good enough just where they are, dumped at the roadside. They are—unwittingly—sculpture. They are Art. They are The Pebbles. 🐌

FACE TO FACE
Theodore F. Wolff

We all keep mementos from our youth, and three of mine are drawings. ❧ One is a sketch of Abraham Lincoln (complete with log cabin) made when I was 9; another a copy of a Michelangelo figure I worked on for at least a week when I was 12; and the third, a charcoal self-portrait I did as a class project in Madison, Wis., when I was 16. ❧

Precious as they are to me (I still remember the excitement of solving the problem of drawing Lincoln's nose and the thrill of seeing the Michelangelo taking shape), I've paid little attention to them these past 20 or so years. They've been in a box with other items from my early days, and they'd still be there if I hadn't decided to haul them out a few days ago for a reappraisal.

I must have spent a good half-hour studying the self-portrait and remembering where I was and what I believed and expected out of life when I drew it. I was particularly intrigued by the strong, positive impression it conveyed. Could that really be me, I wondered, and could I really draw that well in those days?

I felt curiously detached from, and yet somewhat intimidated by, the teenager looking out at me. What, he seemed to be saying, have you done with your life? Were we to meet today, would I *like* you, let alone respect you? Be honest, have you lived up to my expectations, fulfilled the promise of my talent, remained true to my ideals and dreams?

Responding was not easy, for the young man in the picture was a demanding and highly idealistic individual whose closest "friends" were Rembrandt, Michelangelo, and Leonardo, and whose idea of heaven was to stay up all night drawing to the music of Wagner and Sibelius. How could I explain to this intense young perfectionist that while his perception of art may

16

have been good, his understanding of life and human reality were not?

Or was I only making excuses? Trying to divert a potentially painful confrontation by insisting that the unforeseen complications and temptations I had encountered during my lifetime were really beyond my control? Perhaps, but I rather doubt it, for I knew my younger self would see through such a subterfuge and hold me accountable, no matter how I rationalized my life to date.

And besides, I felt rather good about myself. True enough, I might have some difficulty explaining to my young friend why I stopped painting in my early 50s to become an art critic, and why I did a few other things along the way. But all in all, I could look him straight in the eye and tell him that while things may not have turned out quite as he had expected, I had, nevertheless, remained essentially "on course."

Had I really wanted to divert his attention, I could easily have done so by describing all that's happened in art since 1942. That would have thrown him for a loop and taken up many hours of explanation. In 1942 modernism, after all, let alone Abstract Expressionism, hadn't as yet taken over American art, and in the Midwest, especially, painters like John Steuart Curry, Thomas Hart Benton, and Grant Wood were regarded at least as highly as Picasso and Matisse.

I had met Curry and Benton and had recently received short letters from both in response to my request for advice about where to study art. Curry had recommended the University of Wisconsin and had included a landscape sketch (another of my treasured mementos). Benton, on the other hand, scribbled that "any good art school will do. After you've worked hard for 10 years, write me again."

I had just discovered the early drawings and paintings of Picasso, but the joys and mysteries of Cézanne were still two years off for me. And as for such modernists as Miró, Mondrian, and Klee, it would be another four or five years before I would catch on to what they and their colleagues were up to.

I would never, I realized, be able to explain Jackson Pollock's work to my 16-year-old self. He might like it, but he would never accept it as art. And if Pollock was difficult, I dread to think of what I would encounter were I to introduce him to Conceptualism, Earth Art, Body Art, Minimalism, or most of the other movements that erupted and then largely disappeared over the past 40 years.

His rejection of them all would be total and complete—and generally

17

for good, solid traditional reasons. He would represent an excellent case and would make a special point of reminding me that not everything new is good, and that novelty, "originality," and innovative procedures do not necessarily produce art.

For that and several other reasons—most particularly its ability to challenge me to remain true to my ideas and dreams—I've decided to have the self-portrait framed and hung over my desk. Not only will it keep me on my toes, it will also serve as a kind of "spokesman" for those of my readers who have the same difficulties with some of the more extreme forms of modernism and post-modernism my younger self would have today. &

'Who Can Tell The Dancer From The Dance?'
Jamake Highwater

I have been watching choreographers create dances ever since my childhood, when I often visited the studio of the legendary Ruth St. Denis in the San Fernando Valley of Los Angeles. ☙

At 80, Miss Ruth was no longer teaching or performing and had delegated the administration of her school to a young assistant. But now and again, I was fortunate enough to be present on those rare evenings when Miss Ruth came drifting down the stairs from her apartment over the studio.

What a spectacular experience that was! Her tall, lithe figure crowned by a great mass of white hair defied her advanced age. Her charisma was so overwhelming at close quarters that she seemed more specter than person. Her smallest gesture was unexplainably expressive, magnetic, magical.

I had no idea what her movement meant, but I had absolutely no doubt that it was meaningful. It seemed to me, as a youth, that through Ruth St. Denis I experienced the ritual heart of some marvelous and alien religion.

What is it about a great dancer that transforms ordinary gesture into powerful art? How can something as illusive and non-literate as dancing contain a potential for expression that verges on religiosity?

Since my youthful encounters with Ruth St. Denis, I have never ceased to be intrigued by that question. This perplexity about the communicative power of dance is not unique to me. As a whole society, we are probably more mystified by dancing than any other art form.

Undoubtedly, part of our discomfort comes from the fact that we live in a culture in which the body has a terrible reputation. From the earliest days of Western civilization, the abhorrence of the flesh and its association with paganism and evil resulted in the castigation of the body.

The dominant religions of the West officially banned the ritual use of dance as early as the 8th century. For all other peoples of the world, such

19

a situation would be unthinkable. For them, dance is an implicit part of religion. In fact, dancing is indistinct from praying.

Given this bit of history, it is little wonder that tribal people have retained a strong conviction about the power of their bodies, while we of the West gradually became so out of touch with our physical selves that in the 1960s and '70s it was necessary to rediscover our bodies through "consciousness raising" therapy and courses in body language. Eventually many churches reinvented ecclesiastical dancing, and dancers once again became the acrobats of God—a spiritual role they had held in most other civilizations.

For many of us the reemergence of dance as a respectable form of expression did not answer a fundamental question. Why does something as apparently useless and primitive as dance possess such power among most of the world's peoples?

It took many journeys into the heartland of remote nations before I could answer that question. While body movement is unquestionably pleasant to the eye, its real power is more profound than its visual niceties.

Movement communicates. Yawning is an obvious example of its contagion; so is the desire to strech when we see someone else stretching. Because of this inherent quality of motion, which makes onlookers feel in their own bodies the exertion they see in others, the body of the dancer is able "kinesthetically" to convey the most intangible and metaphysical experiences, impressions, feelings, and ideas.

What I discovered among the ritual dancers of Asia, Africa, South America, and Indian America is that the body is capable of communicating in its own language. The choreographer uses that powerful quality of movement to produce an effect upon an audience that achieves an ideal fusion of feeling, form, and thought called "art."

People like Ruth St. Denis managed to understand something that utterly escaped the rest of us. For the dancer, the body is an organ of expression. It is not simply an embarassing and utilitarian network of limbs. It is not just the machinery of procreation, digestion, and other functional activities; it is also an organ of expression—perhaps the most vivid facility for the expression of immediate and strongly felt ideas and feelings.

For holy dancers, the body is the organism in which motion makes visible the sacred forms of life itself. Our bodies live through motion. And thus motion is a most important and pervasive means by which religious rituals celebrate living.

20

The idea that spirituality can be associated with the body is extremely remote from our belief in the dichotomy of mind and body, spirit and flesh. That conviction has made us resist the importance of dance as art.

Until very recently it was inconceivable that there could be any relationship between spiritual and physical realities. To most of us, dances like the ballet and the fox trot or the waltz are, at best, simply pretty, mindless forms of amusement. Only after the turn of the century was dancing changed into a true art by people like Ruth St. Denis, Isadora Duncan, Martha Graham, Erick Hawkins, and Merce Cunningham.

Until the time of these pioneers, dancing was profoundly misunderstood as an activity that was both pointless and profane. Even today, there are many people who look upon dance as a passionate but pointless waste of energy. I recall my foster father's comment at the close of a dance performance, "If those people would just apply all that sweat and effort to hard work, they could really accomplish something." After all, he asked, what does a dance accomplish?

There are as many answers to that question as there are people who create dances. Most choreographers would insist that what a dance achieves is what poetry achieves. It transforms the ordinary into the extraordinary.

Dance changes natural movement into metaphors much the way poetry changes ordinary words so they can mean something that words normally cannot mean. The most curious thing about any art form is its power to insinuate. Sometimes by not saying exactly what we mean, we are able to *imply* exactly what we mean.

That is precisely what Ruth St. Denis did for me many years ago when she turned the descent of a stairway into an unspeakably impressive and memorable experience. She was in such control of her body that she was capable of investing that simple movement with the kind of metaphor that is expressed through poetry.

What does dance accomplish? W. B. Yeats was a poet, so he perfectly understood how powerfully but also how imprecisely art expresses our most sublime thoughts and feelings. It was Yeats who asked: "Who can tell the dancer from the dance?" 🐌

Singing Verdi's Requiem In Concert
April Austin

There's a crossover point at which music becomes more than an assemblage of notes, rests, and dynamic markings. ☙ Somewhere along the rehearsal process—if it was a good one— the struggle to *make* music yields to the power of the music itself. ☙ This was my experience in preparation for a concert of the Verdi "Requiem." ☙ I've done quite a bit of choral singing, but nothing really prepares you for Verdi. ☙ Not with full orchestra and professional soloists. ☙

It was one thing for the choir to rehearse in the confines of our church-basement practice room, with simple piano. Each of us strained to hear the lines of our own part, attempted to mesh with the three other parts, tried to wean ourselves from the score so we could watch our director, the Rev. Larry Hill.

In the first full rehearsal with the orchestra—the musicians were professional, paid by the hour in accordance with union rules—suddenly the comfortable routine was shattered.

As an alto, I stood behind the trombones. Three of them. The rest of the brass and woodwinds were stacked, row by row, in front and to the side of them. When they launched into the "Dies Irae" for the first time, with the crashing rush of demons loosed from hell, I couldn't believe it. I was singing, but my voice was as effectively drowned out as if I was singing underwater.

The mezzo-soprano soloist stood up to sing, and her deep, rich voice cut through the orchestra like a knife through cheesecake. I listened, wondering whether the chorus was ever going to be heard above all the musical pyrotechnics. Fortunately, I've been through this crisis of confidence in preparation for other concerts—orchestras can get carried away, and they have to learn where to play *under* the vocal parts. Our director began to pull the orchestra back.

One by one we worked through the inevitable glitches and mangled lines. Pitches were tuned as we listened for our parts inside the orchestral arrangement and tried to hear our fellow singers. We fought our instinct to retreat back into the written score when we got buried under the orchestra, missing subtle cues and some of our major entrances.

Somewhere along the way, with help from Larry's marvelous hands and the encouragement in his face, we began to expand vocally. We breathed deep from the center of our bodies, felt the music underneath us, buoying us up, carrying us along with potent certainty.

The whole character of the music—Verdi's music—was suddenly illuminated from the inside out. My confidence in our interpretation of the music soared. I heard canyons and mountains in the fugal passages that I hadn't been aware of before. The trombones became heraldic, the bassoons and clarinets seductive. The violins shimmered under long glides of the bow. I couldn't resist the music's pull.

The morning of the concert I woke to vibrations of Verdi in my head. I thought about the 100-odd other chorale members who all must be waking to the "Requiem." Later, I drove to the concert with Verdi going full tilt on the tape deck, singing at the top of my lungs. I dropped the volume only at intersections; it's hard to sing without moving your lips so as not to attract attention.

When I arrived, women in long, black concert dress and men in dark suits jammed the hall, scanning their scores and adjusting ties. Larry took some ribbing for his immaculate tux and tails. Musicians wiped their foreheads and puffed into their instruments. The energy was a palpable tension in the air.

The choir crammed onstage behind the orchestra. The house lights dimmed, and the first cello notes floated across the hall. Music like this, with Verdi's flair for the dramatic, is *felt* as well as heard. The audience hushed, the focus intensified. I felt the hair rise on the back of my neck as the sound welled up and poured over the listeners, saturating them.

The Latin of the requiem mass echoed the resonance of the music. Through the words, allied with the music, I felt the striving of people throughout all ages who struggle for liberation, redemption, and an affirmation of things eternal. 🐚

Rich, Buddy
Roderick Nordell

Buddy Rich and I have two things in common. ❧ We both play drums, and we both belonged to the United States Marine Corps when it was in to be in. ❧

We differ in that I have gone miles to hear Mr. Rich play, while he has never, so far as I know, made any effort to hear me. Also, he has a public pose of ineffable arrogance, which is why they call him Harry Humble, while I have a public pose of kindly forbearance, which may be why nobody calls me.

Obviously one doesn't have to come on like a nice guy to play great drums. So much for conventional wisdom.

When someone has worked and achieved and succeeded, as Mr. Rich has, wouldn't you expect him to be the benign mentor of the young, passing on the torch as it had been passed to him? I took my sons to a drum clinic held by Mr. Rich in Boston not long ago, and when an earnest young questioner asked him how to develop his left hand, Mr. Rich snapped: "Step on it."

Another innocent asked Super Drummer (as he is advertised) if he advised practicing on a practice pad (a rubber mat that permits relatively quiet drumming).

"Going to play a job on a practice pad, practice on a practice pad," grated Mr. Rich. "Going to play a job on a drum, practice on a drum."

How did he think So-and-So (another great drummer) played? "Wrong."

Could he name some drummers he did like? A few, but there seemed to be more good new ones in Britain, where he had just played for the Queen. Not many good ones in America because not many good teachers, he told the audience of students and teachers.

An older man asked if Buddy would tap dance. "I'm not here to give an exhibition."

Of course, Mr. Rich could have tap-danced. And could have sung, too. (Who could forget his way with "I want the frim-fram sauce with the ossinfay—and shifafa on the side"?) Or could have done a complete vaudeville act, like his parents who set their small son up behind the drums as part of their act 50 years ago. (At least once he did have such an act with special materials like "I'm Rich, Buddy—Buddy Rich am I!")

And he did teach people at the drum clinic something in the midst of what he himself called his arrogance. Step on your left hand, he snorted, but then he explained that he tried not to think of it as his left hand, and he tried to be able to do everything with either hand.

How about holding the left-hand stick the same as the right stick in the Ringo Starr manner? No, that's "wrong." The left hand should retain the classic grip, with the stick cradled at the base of thumb and forefinger, extending under the curled second and third fingers, and resting on the fourth and fifth fingers.

Any advice on tuning drums? A curt "you don't tune drums, you tension them." But then, epiphany! He said he tightened the bottom head of his snare drum a little tighter than the top, the reverse of the customary practice.

Did he prefer the heads generally tight or loose? "I like them tight, so everyone can hear my mistakes."

Imagine a hip curmudgeon with a vision of perfection. Beneath all the wise-guy brass was a total professional, someone who was going to get things right.

I began stealing from Bernard (Buddy) Rich in the Swing Era before World War II when he was playing with Artie Shaw, Benny Goodman's main popular rival on the clarinet. Buddy did a pristine fourbar break on the snare drum, with tom-tom punctuation, that seems as clear to me now as it did when I was a schoolboy copying it.

Later there was the night on leave at the Hollywood Palladium when I first saw him in person, playing an unbelievably fast triplet on the cymbal coordinated with his foot pedal on the bass drum. And just this year at the Boston Globe Jazz Festival and the Newport Jazz Festival, I caught up again with his stunning display of speed and precision, shouting "One . . . two . . . three . . ." as he played, to cue in the band he has led for five years now— "the most totally successful band I've ever had in my life," he said on TV's "David Frost Show" this summer.

No display of arrogance with Mr. Frost and guest Raquel Welch. Mr. Rich was all insouciant charm, modestly remarking that his drumming was "not as hard as it looks . . . I just go out and pick up my sticks and play."

25

How about those altercations with various people over the years? Just misunderstandings, Mr. Rich genially told Mr. Frost. What did he mean? "I say something, and they misunderstand it," said Buddy with a grin.

A Rich-watcher couldn't help thinking back to the days when both Mr. Rich and Frank Sinatra were with the Tommy Dorsey band, and their friction (mellowed in recent years) made headlines. One of the things that bothered Mr. Sinatra, according to George T. Simon in his book, "The Big Bands," was the time Mr. Rich persuaded a pretty girl to wait in line for the Sinatra autograph and then say: "Gee, thank you so much, Frankie. Now if I can get just three more of these, I can trade them in for one of Bob Eberly's!" (Bob Eberly! Helen O'Connell! "Tangerine!" There's another story.)

Now my older son is the age I was when I first heard Buddy. I took him out to a roadside jazz club that was having a Buddy Rich matinee for all ages. We couldn't get in. Super Drummer had sold out again.

But we were permitted to stand outside the window behind the bandstand, and we could hear every roll and rimshot cutting through with Buddy's deadly accuracy. I noticed a couple of other men with boys like mine, and when we looked at each other we didn't have to say a thing. 🐚

Into The Hearts Of Thousands
Maggie Lewis

One of my favorite memories is driving home from Oakland to Berkeley at dusk on Mondays and Wednesdays. ❧ I would be humming some jazz I had heretofore been unaware of: Fats Waller, Lester Young, or anything else my tap teacher and heroine, Camden Richman, happened to want us to dance to. ❧ With aching toes, stretched out ankles, and a sprung feeling in my hip sockets, I'd zoom down potholed College Avenue, so named because it ran from the University to the California College of Arts and Crafts. ❧ It also ran from my apartment to Everybody's Dance Studio. ❧ I had signed up for tap dancing in desperation, while being a half-time file clerk and a half-time writer of letters about amazing articles I could produce for various magazines and newspapers. ❧ I drove up College Avenue and back twice a week during an otherwise very boring year and a half. ❧ On the way back, at least, I never felt I was in a rut. ❧ The shabby storefronts flew by and I had a strange affection for them, because after a tap class, I felt I could go anywhere. Broadway, maybe. ❧

Tap gave me, and the other disgruntled office workers in my class, something to strain towards. You knew you probably wouldn't be as magic as Bill Robinson, dancing up the stairs in "Rebecca of Sunnybrook Farm" with a bam on the front of each stair, a click of the heels in the air and a couple of taps on top. Or as ingenuously, fiendishly brilliant as Shirley Temple, dimpling up at him from knee level, getting off the same noises with that little skirt bouncing, and, no doubt, a metronome going in her head (they didn't have computers then) to keep those feet flying to just the right places. And no point even trying to be as graceful as Ginger Rogers, who doesn't even look heavy enough to make all that noise. And who could approach "Fred," as our teacher simply and reverently referred to him?

Maybe tapdancing appealed to us because of all these heroes. They were so arcane. I mean, there are actually quite a few people who don't realize tapdancing is an art. There was a conspiratorial feeling about it, the same feeling little boys who know all the batting averages probably get. A group of us once turned up at the same Fred and Ginger movie and gasped at all the hard steps, which must have annoyed the uninitiated.

But what really kept us coming down the road to Oakland was our teacher. She was an amazing tap dancer. Small, but loosely hung together and skinny so she looked taller, she had an amazingly definite, not to say powerful, way of snapping sounds off the floor with her pointy black shoes that seemed to hang so delicately from frail-looking ankles.

She kept her feet close to the floor when she danced, and encouraged our hero-worship by constant references to the greats—"This is a real Fred you're doing here, so keep your arms out and stay lifted"; or "Bill Robinson was *always* up on his toes. Always. Makes you go so much faster"; or "The Nicholas Brothers could do this six feet in the air, and then land in the splits"; or "The Step Brothers would get *five* taps out of this beat." There was a pantheon being held up to us constantly. But I wonder if Camden knew that she was the main hero among all of them.

She taught all day—she was our age and, like most of us, was doing something secondary to support her True Ambition, which was to become a concert tappist. By the time we all got off work and came to her studio she had taught beginners to near-professionals and had probably taken an excruciating precision-honed class from *her* tapmaster, or rehearsed for some gig somewhere, and her neck tendons were clearly visible. But, stringy as she was, she had a lot of stamina. Singlehandedly, she could bulldoze our group of 25 people's 50 unwieldy feet out of spasms of disconsolate and random thumping into the happy and elegant tattoo she had in mind.

As we stumbled woefully in small groups across the beaten plywood floor, all copying anyone who looked slightly self-confident, she stood in the corner, nodding to the music from the waist up, clapping and watching us eagerly. It was as if she had to pull us across the floor with her eyebrows, she raised them in such strenuous hope and anticipation as she shouted out the steps: "Eight-a-*one*, shuf-fle hop cramproll *stomp* and around! Around! No! Eight-a-*one*, shuf-fle hop cramproll *stomp* and around! No! The other way!"

She had great hope in us. Much more than we ourselves had. Whereas we thought we were just taking tap for a hobby, something to distract us from our typing, filing, waiting on tables, or computer programming, she would never admit that any one of us couldn't aspire to "Fred" status. She did herself, and she just couldn't imagine tap-dancing as a mere pastime.

Her belief in us was unremitting. It was just as powerful as if she had shot pistols at our feet and shouted "dance!" as in a Western movie. And sometimes it was almost as uncomfortable. No matter how much a new step reminded you of climbing sheer granite cliffs in socks, no matter if you had to make more sounds than you could even count in the space of one saxophone toot, whenever you looked up from your noisy, recalcitrant feet, there she'd be in the corner of the room, clapping and raising her eyebrows and vibrating with promise. It was *your* promise she was concentrating on. So you'd helplessly stumble on. Annoying as it could be, she Knew You Could Do It. And, after what seemed like a forty-mile hike back and forth across the floor, you could, suddenly.

We got better. Some dropped out of the class, but there were many of us who had come in together as Tap I, not knowing anything, and shambled around with our taps clonking self-consciously, and who, after a very long time and suffering many toe splints, knew single, double, and triple time steps with a Bill Robinson break, and Maxie Fours with pickups. Some of us showed up for class one day when it was 103 degrees just to see if we could do it. We were renamed Tap II and were unbearably proud, though none of our friends outside the class could understand.

Elsewhere in my life, I was misfiling important documents and getting rejection letters. But in Tap II on Monday and Wednesday nights, I was moving—with a progress perceptible only to Camden—Fredward. I never got there. I got a newspaper job and moved. I don't have to file any more, and I'm getting published, and I realize I wasn't really going to be a tap-dancer, but sometimes I wish I was still on the way. ❦

An Interview With Painter Wolf Kahn
Michael Huey

O n the road near Brattleboro, Vermont. 🐗 Late autumn. 🐗 Low clouds activate the sky. 🐗 When they expose the sun the northern horizon turns dark as asphalt, small stands of trees luminesce, and fade. 🐗

There is a fire in the wood stove of Wolf Kahn's house when I arrive. He has been working on a pastel sketch of a view from the front window: out over a small slope where they're building him a new studio (its fresh plywood a Naples yellow in the sketch), a row of maples, warm dark distant hills. As he looks from the window to the sketch, Wolf Kahn talks about how the shifting light compels him to work.

Do artists see things other people don't? Is the artist a prophet?

I like to make small claims. Van Gogh saw colors, undoubtedly, that no one else saw. It didn't take the rest of the world very long to catch up to him, however. Now everybody sees colors the way he did. He saw the landscape sort of rippling across in ribbons, and it didn't take very long for everyone to be aware that the landscape was composed of rippling ribbons. I think the artist focuses things for people.

When you're painting well, are you outside yourself?

I think the best painting is done when there's enough paint on your canvas that the picture tells you what to do and you don't have to tell the picture a thing. All you have to do is answer the questions that the picture asks. Hopefully the picture asks the questions that you ask of nature, and they get answered in your picture. Such as, "What kind of connections are there? What's separate, what's together?" Things like that.

And if you're not painting well are you more aware of your emotion? Does painting ever make you angry?

I try to be toward my work the way a carpenter feels about making a table. To be severe, but workmanlike, without asking any highfalutin questions. When he's making a table, the carpenter doesn't ask, "What's the function of a table?" He tries to make a table that doesn't wobble. He tries to make a table that's the right height. All kinds of very down-to-earth sort of things that should [also] happen in a picture. Anything else that comes along comes along unbidden but often welcome.

Tell me about finding a direction of your own.

I never tried to find a way of my own, I never *tried* to be original. I was never afraid to be influenced by, and to steal from anybody whose work I was fond of. I still do. A lot of times I see somebody who's younger than I and I steal from him or her, because I think there's something that's worth appropriating. That's how a culture is formed, by people stealing from each other. No disgrace in it. The disgrace, I think, lies in this frantic search for originality, which is apt to bring forth abominations.

Where are you in your career?

I'm in a place in my career where things are going easier and better all the while, and at the same time I'm not a celebrity. I'm not Andy Warhol, nor do I wish to be. My privacy is only very infrequently invaded, such as by you, and so every time it happens I rather like it.

I think it's very problematical to be a landscape painter in this day and age. But I try not to let that influence me, and I push it way aside when I do my work.

And yet, one pays the price for that, too. Museum people and critics tend to look at my work and say, "Well, this is just wall furniture," and, "It's all been done before," and of course that saves them a lot of trouble. They don't actually have to look at the paintings then. To look at the paintings you have to have feelings, you have to have ideas, you have to understand the tradition. You have to see in what way I go beyond the tradition, that I do paintings that have never been done before, and so on. Most of them don't understand that.

How you go beyond the tradition?

It's not one of my concerns to go beyond the tradition. I love the tradition and I would be perfectly happy just to be "one of the workers in the vineyard" who helps keep the thing going. But I think I do go beyond it in *color*. Because I use much wilder colors than, say, the Impressionists used.

Is that what it means to be a colorist?

Colorist just means that you have a good color sense and you use color in a way that's arresting. That again is like a gift. It's sort of like having a good voice.

I read somewhere that you once said, "I'm always trying to get to a danger point in color." Can you explain that?

Danger point means that people aren't used to it. If somebody comes along and says, "That painting's too sweet," it means that they can't deal with the fact that you're doing a set of color relations that actually they've seen last on a candy package. Or a perfume ad. And yet, you're not doing a perfume ad, you're doing a painting. And a painting has to represent your most deeply considered sense of life. Which is, that it has to have a sense of gravity to it, contrast, austerity. When you're getting to danger points, you're working in fairly new ground, and you can be having quite a hard time of it. And you're aware that you're skirting, all the time skirting, the possible.

Is it hard for you to look at your early work?

No, I rather like my early work. It's much more difficult for me to look at the work I did yesterday, because that's still filled with anxiety, and fear and doubt, and so forth. Things that I did 20 years ago I look at now and say, "Gee, how come I was so worried at the time I was doing those? They look pretty good."

What were you worried about? What do you fear now?

You always fear the same thing, which is that you're not good enough, and that you're trying to get away with something, and that what you have to say isn't worth saying. This business of being an artist isn't a joke, because you've been given leave by the world at large to do something that other people do as a hobby and to do it seriously and to sustain yourself and your family by it, financially. And that puts a burden on you. You can't just do it for fun anymore. It's like being a major-league baseball player. It's no longer just a game, but it becomes something that has anxiety and tension attached to it.

What role does spontaneity play in your work? Is it fostered by your spending half the year here in Vermont?

There has to be a true response to the unique moment. Of course, being out of the studio, out in nature, is very helpful to that end, because each moment is so different. You're fresh. You're new. You're going to learn something that you didn't know before, you're going to do something that you haven't done before.

It's not as easy to do that in the studio, because there the only thing that you have to get your imagination and juices flowing is the color and the medium and maybe a few sketches. And the sketches might be holding you back. When you're out there in front of nature you see the mess that nature presents. The organized elements that you do find, that you clamp onto for dear life in the face of this chaos—those organized elements are exactly what you don't want in your painting, because that's all stuff that's predigested, that everybody knows about.

Namely that a tree has green leaves, or that there's a line where the road goes through the field, or that, as you look into the distance things get bluer. You want me to read what I wrote about that?

Go ahead.

"Innocence of spirit is what's called for at all times. It alone allows you to take risks, because they're not perceived as risks. Anything which you perceive as risky makes you careful, and I love painting which doesn't hold back."

Do you work differently in New York than here?

Well, I don't work directly from nature in New York, of course. And I tend to be more synthetic in my work.

I try to deal with the underlying idea of a painting in my studio in New York, whereas here I'm much more interested in getting information; not information in the sense of cataloging a whole lot of twigs and branches, but information in the deep sense, relating my canvas to my field of vision in a way where people know that I was there.

That means, again, spontaneity and the ability to see things for what they really are. If you really see the color of trees, they're not green, they change with the light. You have to be quick on your feet to catch that. If you're not interested in actually catching it, then you have to find some sort of equivalence for your experience in nature. And that's where it's good to be away from nature, to be off in your studio.

There's a statement by Wordsworth, the English poet, who said that "Art is emotion recollected in tranquillity." Famous statement. Well, I say that I find Vermont much too emotional. I find New York very tranquil. Paradoxes abound in art as in life. 🐘

Interview With Sculptor George Rickey
Susan Carlson

The house is on a hill in the Berkshires. ❧ As I drive closer I suddenly see the glint of giant silver blades, moving slowly, beyond the garden. ❧ They look like planets revolving in a stainless steel solar system suspended from a wire between two trees. ❧

When I turn into George Rickey's driveway I see a lawn glittering with rectangular forms that seem to wave a welcome. I have entered another world and can't keep from smiling.

The green and breezy outdoors is Mr. Rickey's gallery. He has cut away the underbrush around the house and beyond the small patio. To one side, a simple fixture harnesses a trickle of spring water to create a waterfall, a melodic, spouting backdrop for an interview.

Shortly after I arrive, Rickey suggests a tour of the grounds. On the way he points out the newly installed "Triple N," a towering series of silver angles that took a year to make. It stands grandly among the trees in the side yard, moving constantly to the rhythm of the wind.

We set off down the driveway and across the road past numerous sculptures to Hand Hollow Brook. ("They instruct me," the artist says of his work.) A path leads from the brook to a pond and a clearing enhanced with sculptures. They appear to "float" in the water and in the grass.

On one side, a building resembling a small airplane hangar houses more of Rickey's work. The walls of the shop are covered with tools, many hand-made by the artist. He says, "Let me poke," as he takes a rod, turns and sets a work in motion.

A friendly man with gentle eyes and a ready smile, the artist, a poet in the world of motion, began making kinetic sculpture in 1949. "I wanted to make art in which movement was a component," Rickey explains. "I had been a painter for 20 years. I wasn't after movement and turned it into art. We're all involved with movement, concerned with it, able to perceive it. Art had been without it except for the dance."

We watch the sculpture move. "I'm interested in arranging movement so there are near-misses," Rickey remarks. "When there are near-misses, there's an element of anxiety—will they hit or not? I know from reading novels that this has been a part of storytelling. Without anxiety you wouldn't have the novel."

"So there needs to be suspense in sculpture, too?" I ask.

"Yes," the sculptor replies, "but if you overdo it, it's a bore. Part of it is to have the performance contrary to expectation. Yet it is all completely logical; it is not just a game.

"One trouble with motor-driven pieces," Rickey continues, "is that with very few exceptions they repeat. Once it repeats, it's like yesterday's newspaper. So long as it is random, one cannot tell just what is coming up. And so there is *expectancy,* which I think is very important in art."

All of Rickey's sculptures move according to the principle of compound or simple pendulums, based on a fulcrum, a stiff rod, and a lead counterweight. He explains: "The fulcrum is the shaft, lead is used as a counterweight, and the stiff blade functions as a rod. Planes and open geometric shapes can also be mounted to behave as pendulums."

In discussing these shapes, he describes a tetrahedron. "It has four faces and each face is a triangle. It's an extremely stable form, very strong. I've used it as a basic form. At the back of that is wanting shapes that are in themselves extremely simple, not in any way romantic, absolutely without interest. They are only of interest when they move."

Walking among the sculptures, I notice their surfaces, which are burnished. "I work the surface in order to make it visible," explains the artist. "If a surface is moving, its relationship to a light source is constantly shifting. So there's a certain dynamism on the surface. A little movement reflects a lot. I'm not trying to make abstract painting. I just want it to react."

Back in his workshop he points out various three-dimensional studies for sculptures, all of them, naturally, a fraction of the size of the works outdoors. "I've been undertaking things that seem impossible," he comments. "I've got pieces here that are double-jointed, and one with five joints. They are created to move as slowly as possible and still remain stable." (Sometimes Rickey calls on the assistance of an engineer who tells him such things as how big bolts must be to withstand 80 m.p.h. winds.)

35

"I'm rather square compared to Calder," Rickey admits. "There's a great deal of humor in his work, wit and playfulness. I'm really much more serious. I'm concerned with a certain lyricism, but not with anything jokey. Calder often did things quite jokey.

"I don't want to do anything for effect, or just to engage attention. It's not theater here. The question is: Can one do something that seems visually worth doing? And get the materials organized to permit it to happen. That's my occupation."

The artist continues with the startling remark: "I don't care what the sculptures look like, because I can always adjust the shapes. I may decide to make them wider and flatter or tapered or not tapered. I may make changes in the shape, dictated by the weight I can allow myself."

After our tour of the sculptures Rickey's wife Edith serves lunch on the patio. Over ham and cucumber sandwiches, fresh green beans and home-grown tomatoes, we discuss the part time plays in Rickey's work.

"The component of time is in music always," he notes, "but in the visual arts it's been bypassed. It's in dance, of course, but in drawing, painting and design the concept of time is absent. Also the time to be given by the observer/viewer, *that* is absent. Part of my interest is to slow it all down.

"If you've watched a sculpture for ten seconds, you haven't yet seen it. It is self-renewing, random. The viewer has to give it time. Otherwise he gets nothing.

"Movement is of constant interest, like sitting on a beach and watching the waves. Perceiving movement requires no training. With a great deal of modern art you have to have a good deal of preparation for it. You have to discover what the idiom is. What are the agreed-on rules of the game? Movement is the most universal of experiences, yet little exploited as a means."

I ask about Rickey's observations of the current art scene.

He smiles and shakes his head. (Or: He shrugs expressively.) "In the last generation," he says, " 'fashion' in art has increased enormously. It imitates the fashion in clothing; it's virtually seasonal now. If you go down to SoHo or West Broadway, in New York, there will be discussion there and in the press —What's art doing this year? What's it going to be this fall? I think what's new is irrelevant." He smiles. "Sometimes art is good in spite of being new."

He continues, "Some artists are just out to capture attention for themselves. To trap attention. What's *lyrical* is not to attract attention. It hopes to be seen and heard, but it is not done for effect.

36

"Arthur Schopenhauer wrote of acts of will without motive or any attempt to manipulate. Just action of itself. The idea is that something can want to become, to be born, just of itself. Not because something else requires it.

"According to Schopenhauer the concern of art is with *contemplation,* or will-less perception. The aesthetic frame of mind is characterized by a complete absence of desire or practical interest. And that's very close to what I think. My work is very much something that is just made. The making is all of it."

Returning to the idea of movement, Rickey explains how, using paper and pencil for calculating, he decides what to do with weight, distance, and shape to get a perfect balance. The result is a slowness and smoothness of movement that has much to teach the observer who is willing to watch and learn.

"You have to come to a definition of your problem," he says. When asked what he sees as his problem he replies: "Why, this: is it possible?"

What is possible may be seen on the hillsides and in the forest near his home, and in galleries, gardens, and public places around the world. After walking around the grounds and work areas, one becomes acutely aware of the problem-solving these sculptures represent. The artist and his work are in full swing, in every sense of the word. 🐚

TALE OF A TEA BOWL
Jane Brown Bambery

It was another rainy day in Tokyo. For me, a tourist, that meant postponing—again—a day trip to Mt. Fuji and its celebrated views. I was disappointed, but gathered my rain gear and went out to explore more of Tokyo instead.

Soon I was ducking the rain on the Ginza, Tokyo's Madison Avenue, jostled by a sea of bristling umbrellas. Without quite knowing why, I suddenly found myself staring into a very posh gallery window, as elegant and chic as many I had already passed, but this time I was transfixed. Despite the waves of umbrellas breaking dangerously on either side, I stopped short to gaze at a tea bowl displayed by itself under a single track light.

Only about four inches high and the same diameter, this tiny tea bowl had a creamy white glaze with an intricately pitted surface—like baked meringue just starting to separate. The glaze showed traces of rusty brown here and there, perhaps from some impurities in the glazing compound, giving the impression that it had started to turn golden-brown in the oven. Yet these irregularities, like a birthmark on a beautiful face, seemed to enhance the bowl's exquisite features all the more by setting them off. I was drawn inside.

As I stood looking down on the object, occasionally shifting my stance to view it from a different perspective, the tea bowl assumed the changeable character of a landscape. From the side its profile resembled an old mountain: fissured by rivers long and dry; experienced; rounded by time.

It was the skin of the bowl, though, that seen through slightly squinted, unfocused eyes, suggested unlimited changing scenes, one dissolving into the next: First it was the brittle surface of polar ice with spots of tundra peeking through. That image melted into an expanse of scorched desert dunes, then washed into a froth of ocean foam on soaked sand, then solidified as the cool, uneven surface of the moon. Then for a moment the glaze took on the soft sheen of an antelope hide, white and porous. Looking directly down into the pool of the bowl, I stared for an instant into the mouth of an ancient cave where humankind's earliest dramas were played out.

These images flowed one from another for several seconds in a sort of meditation, with no thought to the human endeavor that had created them. Finally I stepped back, seeing the clay teacup as itself once more, stark and humble under the track light. How did the artist infuse such life, so much of the world into a small, inanimate object?

Later, back in my hotel, I stopped in the bookstore to buy some post-cards. A pocket guide called "Japanese Ceramics," with its pretty cover design of a red, blue, and white Imari plate, caught my eye. Reading it in my room as the rain coursed down the windowpane, I found this passage under the heading "Transient Beauty":

"Ceramics are fired at a high temperature, and when they are fired they pass through the singular process of having destroyed in a moment the time they had hitherto experienced and the history they had received in that period . . . The transformation by heat which goes beyond artificial creative intent is heavy with the Far Eastern resignation that 'nothing can be done,' and it is in this changing of the form . . . that the philosophy of quiet taste and weathered simplicity may be born."

And so it was. The tea bowl in the gallery had once been soft, nubile clay, transformed by ravaging fires to emerge hardened, experienced, with a more mature softness and a worldly beauty. A new integrity shown through the small scars and impurities rendered in the kiln, that of a whole greater than the sum of its parts. Achieved intentionally, but not achievable through intent alone—this was the secret that had melded spirit and object. Enriched by such a spirit, any object, no matter how small, could become grand.

How far removed from our modern Western notions that divorce function from beauty, allowing us to choose plastic over ceramics, fast-food over food that pleases the eye and the palate. In a culture of disposable objects, it is no wonder we have created special repositories for art and relegate spiritual life to houses of worship.

As we segregate ourselves further

and further from the spirit which infuses the object, it becomes easier to glory in the large, powerful world we shape through our own intent, completely ignoring influences beyond our control—a fluke of physics, a whim of nature, the caprice of a spirit larger than our own. Our reality is reduced to that which we create and control. All else—aesthetics, emotion, faith—belongs to a realm of dreams and dreamers, too unpredicatable to be "of use" in a practical world.

All this went through my mind as I watched the gray waves tossing in Tokyo Bay through the window of my hotel room. And I took heart that on the rainy Ginza my own Western sensibility had been suddenly brought up short, called to notice that the power and beauty of the world can be contained in a teacup. 🐚

THE THINGS
OF NATURE

Nature Study
Virginia Graham

I have never understood the attraction of bird watching. 🐦 I am prepared to concede there is a certain interest in identifying different species of bird, in being able to exclaim sotto voice: "Look! A bunting!" or "Psst! Isn't that a lesser crested warbler?" 🐦 But after that, unless one is a professional ornithologist, interest is bound, I feel, to flag. 🐦 For birds don't seem to *do* anything very much. 🐦 Not British birds at any rate. 🐦 True, in foreign places, where behavior, as we know, is notoriously lax, birds go in for elaborate courting rituals and even decorate their nests with flowers and ribbons; but in this country we don't hold with such excesses, and in avian matters, as in others, we are demure. 🐦

So our prim, inhibited birds are, to the amateur spectator, terrifically boring to watch. I once spent a whole afternoon in Kensington Gardens, which is where Peter Pan hung out and so is full of innocence, studying the mores of our feathered friends. And honestly they did not offer me sufficient variety in the entertainment line to warrant the time I spent with them. Some of them hopped, some of them ran, some of them flew, and some of them, the pigeons, waddled.

This to my mind, is not enough. I mean, I know birds do these things: During my life I have observed them doing so. I have also noted them flying by with bits of straw and grass and feathers and old bits of toffee paper in their beaks, on their way to fashion these into nests, and I do not see how my friends can spend days, binoculars jammed to their eyes, watching these familiar activities.

However, the certain hardness, or at any rate bewilderment with which I have viewed bird watching in the past has been slightly tempered by a recent experience. Needless to say this weakness in my resolve to stay aloof from birds manifested itself on the Continent—terrible the way everything goes to pieces when one leaves one's native shores; all those dollops of cream on everything and taking siestas and buying table mats one doesn't need. As I was saying, my change of view about birds occurred when I reluctantly, cynically even, held out a crumb to a Bavarian sparrow, and it took it out of my hand.

My traveling companion was, I discovered, an inveterate bird feeder, which is, of course, infinitely worse than being a bird watcher, since it has all the marks of eccentricity. Why this is I know not, but the fact remains that in England women who feed birds—in public that is, for in private it is quite the thing to have an upturned coconut in one's garden with a tomtit hanging upside down on it—in public, as I say, a bird-feeding female is quite likely to be talking to herself or wearing a funny hat.

My fears that our desire to enter the Common Market might be jeopardized by my friend's scattering crumbs round every café table we sat at were voiced in no uncertain terms, but she paid no heed and went on throwing bits of extremely expensive mille-feuilles and sacher tortes to the ground. The birds flocked, of course, and as, through shame, my eyes were lowered, they inevitably alighted on a sparrow who was leaning nonchalantly against my ankle. Urged by my friend, who was sure this grossly overweight bird had taken up this position because it was fainting from hunger, I rolled up a pellet of cake and apathetically offered it to the creature. It took it. From between my fingers.

"Oh," I said, stiff-lipped but with my heart melting.

I have not had time fully to analyze why it is that a bird eating out of my hand should have such a melting effect; but I suspect that it is because it proves what I have long suspected, which is that I am blatantly, patently trustworthy. It seems even a sparrow can sense I am as harmless as its cousin the dove, knows it can place its life, or at any rate its beak, in my gentle hands. And that, of course, is very endearing.

Trying to stick to the advice that one should do in Rome as the Romans do, and this I still firmly believe, includes *not* dotting a café terrace with hundreds of twittering birds, I restrained myself from feeding my sparrow, hand to mouth, more than three times more. In my hotel bedroom, however, which had a French window leading onto a balcony, all my preconceived notions, both on standards of behavior abroad and bird watching, went completely to pot. Every morning my entire breakfast, rolled into pellets, peppered the floor from window to bed, and through it weaved, hopped, and skidded, for the floor was parqueted, enough birds to stock an aviary at a zoo. Most of them were sparrows, and I was able to observe with some astonishment that not all sparrows look alike. Also that some are braver than others. The ones who were tame enough to be fed by hand were the thin, pale, knock-kneed variety, whereas the poltroons, though vociferous, were the fatter, darker feathered breed. I made a note of this and have sent it to the British Ornithological Society.

The wooing and winning of birds is a delicate matter: The breath has to be held, the hand holding the croissant lowered gently. Or so I thought. I was just beginning to congratulate myself on my affinity with St. Francis of Assisi when it was clearly proved to me that some birds think this slow business of learning to love and trust a human being is a sheer waste of time. At any rate there is one bullfinch in Germany who believes it to be a lot of sentimental twaddle. For while I was so carefully, so solicitously courting my sparrows, it flew in at the window, landed without a by-your-leave in the very middle of my plate, threw a few pieces of marmalade over its shoulder, ate half a roll in a businesslike manner, skidded up on the butter, and flew out again.

I confess I was shocked to the core. Such arrogance! I have never liked brash, cocksure, throwing-their-weight-about people, and it was dismaying to find that in ornithological circles this type also exists. This sort of do-it-first-ask-questions-later attitude is one which I, along with democracy, have been fighting all my life, and to find it held by a bullfinch! The cheek of it! It is not exactly that I want bullfinches to cringe, or beg, or plead for crumbs; but I do think they should *ask:*

I am rather furious because all bird watching has done for me, as far as I can see, is to accentuate the similarity between birds and men.

I think I shall go back to watching football. &

44

THE BEE
Glenn Wasson

I've always respected nature as much as the next fellow, but when there's work to be done, I've not been easily diverted, for I was pretty sure man would still be living in caves if he had not learned that the weak had been provided for the benefit of the strong. ❧ But several weeks ago, I had an experience that shook this Darwinian concept of mine. ❧

I had been working hard clearing brush for several hours in the mountains and decided to reward myself with a sandwich. Sitting down on a log, I unwrapped the sandwich and surveyed the rugged scenery around me. It was a familiar scene of natural beauty, but one of which I never tired. Two turbulent mountain streams joined to form a clear, deep pool before roaring down a cataract into a heavily wooded canyon. My idyll would have been perfect had it not been for a persistent bee that became attracted to my sandwich. She was of the common variety that plagues picnickers and buzzes around open garbage containers. Without thinking, I brushed her away.

Not in the least intimidated, she came back and settled on the exact spot on the sandwich that I was about to bite. This time I shook her off and batted her to the ground. Before she could recover, I ground her into the sand with my cleated boot.

A few moments later I was startled by a minor explosion of sand at my feet and my tormentor emerged from what I thought had been her final resting place with her wings buzzing furiously. This time I took no chances. I stood up and ground her into the sand with all my 210 pounds.

Satisfied that this was indeed the *coup de grace,* I once more sat down to enjoy the rest of my lunch. After several minutes I became aware of a slight movement near my feet. A broken but still living bee was feebly emerging from the compacted sand.

Beguiled by her remarkable survival, I leaned down to survey the damage. As she weakly flexed her broken wings I could see that her right wing had several fragments missing from the edges, though it was relatively intact. The left wing, however, was crumpled like a crushed piece of paper and had gaping holes in it. Nevertheless, the bee kept exercising her wings slowly up and down as though she were assessing the damage. Her thorax and abdomen were still encrusted with sand and she began to groom herself.

Next she turned her attention to the crumpled left wing, rapidly smoothing it out by running her legs down the length of it. After each straightening session she buzzed her wings as if to test the improvement in the lift. This hopeless cripple thought she could still fly!

By now she had completely captured my attention, and I got down on my hands and knees to better see her futile attempts at rehabilitation. Closer scrutiny confirmed my earlier assumption; she was finished—she *must* be finished. I reminded myself that my judgment on these matters was not to be taken lightly. After all, I was a veteran pilot myself, and know a good deal about the principle of wings. I had experienced a thousand flights beyond the understanding of her rudimentary senses.

But the bee paid no attention to my superior wisdom; if anything she seemed to be gaining strength and increasing the tempo of her repairs. By repeatedly stroking her crumpled left wing she was gradually restoring its original shape. The broken veins that stiffened the gossamer wing were nearly straight now, but I saw no way for her to restore the gaping holes. Then she did a remarkable thing. She flattened the wing out on the sand and by contorting her lower abdomen over it, began to emit a clear, viscous fluid.

Like a model-plane enthusiast doping fabric over wing spars, she carefully glazed over the missing portions of the wing. The emitted material must have dried quickly, because she began to trial-buzz her wings almost immediately. Time after time she added a bit of her special adhesive here and there to correct what she sensed was needed for strength and balance.

At last the bee felt sufficiently confident to attempt a trial flight. With an audible buzz she released her grip on the earth and flew straight into a slight rise in the sand not more than three inches away. She hit so hard she actually tumbled. More frantic smoothing and flexing of the wing followed. She continued to twist her stinger over the wings to deposit the fluid, but in noticeably more delicate dosage.

46

Once more she lifted off and flew parallel to the ground for about six inches before she hit another small mound of sand. Apparently she had regained the lift in her wings but had not mastered the unfamiliar feel of the directional controls. Each flight was straight ahead, and she hit objects that could have been easily avoided by a slight change in direction. Like a pilot learning the peculiarities of a strange airplane, she experimented with short hops that ended ignominiously in rough, unplanned landings. After each crash landing she worked furiously to correct the newly discovered deficiencies in the wing structure.

Again she took off, this time clearing the small irregularities in the sand but headed straight toward a stump. Narrowly avoiding the stump, she checked her forward speed, circled, and then drifted slowly over the mirror-like surface of the pool as if to admire her own reflection. As she disappeared from sight, I realized that I was still on my knees, and I remained on my knees for some time. 🐖

THE RACCOON SHRUGGED
Rushworth M. Kidder

The other day I had a staring match with a raccoon. 🐾 Or at least that's what *I* thought. 🐾 He probably thought he was invisible—gazing out through his black mask from the dense hazel bushes along the shore, motionless before the green and alien presence of my canoe. 🐾

A moment before, I had come around the point into the marshy shallows. Through the wisps of early morning mist that rose from the lily pads, I had noticed a movement in the bushes. But there was no hint of wind in the Maine sky. The water lay smooth and pearly, like the inside of a mussel shell. So I let the canoe drift and peered, Moses-like, at the bushes, trying to puzzle out the cause of the sudden tuggings and snappings among the leaves. Now and then a paw emerged. Here and there, past gaps in the natural hedge, a banded tail flitted past. And at last, as though assembled into a whole by a force beyond us both, the entire animal appeared near a piece of driftwood. Thirty yards away, my canoe creaked gently against some reeds. We both froze —I with the paddle across the gunwales, he with a forefoot on the log.

One can pass a lot of time watching animals. It's an old and honorable tradition, especially in a country conceived as a frontier and dedicated to the proposition that self-sufficiency rewards those who understand the ways of the wild. But before long, the mind wants more than just a stare. If you're an Audubon, I suppose, you begin to focus on visual detail. If you're a Darwin, you think about phylum and class. If you're a Thoreau, you reflect on the way nature holds an unflattering mirror up to humanity. But what if you're just a journalist on holiday? Raccoons rarely make headlines. And even a solid feature story on the *Procyon lotor,* small cousin of the black bear, would want to dwell on its relationship with people—overturned garbage cans, midnight raids on the compost heap, and that sort of thing. Not much newsworthy in a backwoods stare—at least, not as the world counts newsworthiness.

The canoe, still drifting slightly, swung in a dead-slow arc. I had to move my head gradually, owl-fashion, to keep him in view. The longer I sat there, the more I wondered what it all meant. In a sense, of course, he was just what I wanted: He was my reward for fumbling out of bed before dawn and paddling through the gelid air. I, however, was distinctly not what he expected— an interruption of his otherwise leisurely forage along a hidden stretch of bog. What gave me the right, then, to satisfy my curiosity at the expense of his breakfast? What could I learn from him in person (if the term may be stretched to cover coons) that I couldn't have learned more quickly, and certainly more warmly, by reading about him beside the fire back at the cabin?

It's a matter, I thought (still staring: neither of us had flinched), of privacy. In a way, that's what the call of the wild has always been: the search for seclusion, for sanctuary, for the place far from the eye of society where inner and outer lives become one and each can be lived on the surface. We have friends up here who, when they go camping every summer, set as their only goal the finding of a place as far away from anyone else as they can. That, too, is an old tradition, probably predating Odysseus.

The canoe, by now, had stopped moving. And I began to glimpse, through the black mask of that patient face, what troubled me. This old tradition of seclusion, it seemed, was squarely at odds with journalism. For journalism wants in so many ways to barge in upon that privacy, hale it into public for all the world to see, roll it about on the tongue as the hard candy of the worldly wise. On one hand, the uninvaded wilderness; on the other, the intrusive nose of reportage.

Had it not been for what happened next, I might have left the matter at that—bathing myself in the mixed light of a righteous indignation blended with a slight occupational shame.

But the raccoon suddenly turned away—I'm sure I only imagined that he shrugged—and took up his bushy hunt again. Perhaps he had grown used to my stillness. Or perhaps he had concluded (quite rightly) that a man in a straw hat armed only with paddles at 30 paces was a threat worthy of supreme indifference. But just maybe, knowing he was being watched, he consciously set out to display raccoonishness (or is it raccoonicity?) in its best possible light—assiduously tipping up logs, hunting under tufts, and fishing through the pickerel weed with a new-found determination.

So had I really intruded upon a privacy? Or had I merely watched nature at work? Was I uncovering secrets best left undiscovered? Or was I simply bearing witness to the inherent and instructive characteristics of a neighbor? Was this an invasion or an invitation—and, whichever it was, did it make the world a worse or a better place?

One is not usually driven out of swamps by moral wrestlings. But as I paddled home to breakfast, I realized that there, in that indifferent stretch of woods, I had stumbled upon the central dilemma of the reporter's craft. The good reporter—or essayist, or teacher, or artist of any sort—leaves, like that raccoon, no promising stone unturned. Every detail moves toward coherence. Each gesture and word, however haphazard, begins to compose a character—and, through that, a world. All is grist for the mill.

But with curiosity must come also discretion—the sensitivity that knows when insight has crumbled into mere gossip, how the noble observation of ideas can degenerate into a petty fascination with personalities, where to draw the line between genuine public discourse and legitimately private intimacies. To maintain the highest regard for the confidential, and the lowest tolerance for the cover-up; to write not simply so that the reader can *know* but can *understand;* to do it all without being manipulated by one's subjects or duped by one's own excitement—there are days, I thought as I beached the canoe at the cabin, that it's easier to be a raccoon. What they find, after all, they simply eat—whether or not anyone is watching. 🐾

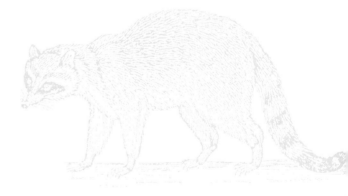

We Are All Only Visiting
Elisavietta Ritchie

"Did you know you have ants in your kitchen?" the scientist asked rather testily. ❧ He was invading the little littered kitchen of my cottage on the briny Patuxent River. ❧

"Ants? So we do!" I screwed the lids more tightly onto the jars which my 11-year-old Alexander had as usual neglected to shut properly. The ants continued their unperturbed journey across the counter. But only a dozen, in single file, and small.

"Don't you have any spray?" persisted my friend, keeping his distance. He was not, thanks, entomologically oriented.

"Spray? Yes, I must put it on my list." I turned over an outdated scrap of paper, which, since it also bore scratches of some nascent poem, probably would never make it to the supermarket. Out of practice with one-stop shopping, after a year of dozens of different multicolored Asian shops and stalls, I doubted I would make it to the supermarket soon, either. Too much cultural shock, embarrassing riches. As for chemical sprays—"For reasons of hygiene—" the scientist was saying.

"These are *country* ants," my son interjected. "*Their* feet don't pollute."

The scientist gave us a disapproving look and went off to examine the latest issue of an astronomy magazine. Up *there,* at least, it was bug free.

I scolded Alexander, in Malay, for arguing with an adult. Malay, which we had both studied in the Far East, had become our secret language.

I gave the ants a disapproving look too; perhaps this might drive them away. It did. Or at least, they were retreating toward a crack in the wall without glancing over their shoulders.

Alexander and I went out into the soft September night to look at the stars. A nighthawk flapped off downriver toward the Chesapeake Bay. Strange to see maples and cedars instead of palms and banana trees. Under our feet, collectives of ants were perhaps closing up for the night.

The first time we had ants indoors here was three years ago. My visiting sister-in-law seemed to feed her children nothing but chocolate and jam. I'd been as horrified by their diet as by the ensuing armies of ants. It took months, subsequently, to get those ants to depart. We had not liked them much.

Now, after a year of living in a village in Malaysia, we had learned to coexist with ants. Indeed, could we have lived as well without them?

Friends had warned Malaysia had too many insects. Some 800 species of butterflies, that was fine, and 200 dragonfly kinds. But all those just plain *bugs*?

And fancy ones. Yet despite some huge emerald beetles which thudded against the lights on August evenings, several foot-long but harmless well-armored millipedes, fiercer and furry wasps with orange cummerbunds, and a cockroach who sat on the other dining chair while I wrote, our household seemed self-debugging.

Hens at the threshold of our wooden house on stilts pecked up or at whatever crawled. The resident praying mantis deleted mosquitoes. At night the toad came up the drainage pipe to stand, or rather hop, guard.

All scorned, or respected, or merely ignored, the ants. But the ants were equally important in the hierarchy of housekeeping.

Usually just a few sparse patrols crossed tables and walls and corridors, acting as scavenger units. Their rewards for continued vigilance: some hapless bug, inevitable crumbs, and a quick trip around the bottle of honey from coconut flowers. Alexander again.

Sometimes great phalanxes of ants traveled like magical carpets over the floor, liquid tapestries across the walls. They knew what they were doing, where they had to go, and the rewards. Our reward: fascination of watching.

Now, beneath the humid stars of another hemisphere, I realized that Alexander's carelessness might, however unconsciously, be a knowledge that one should share with all creatures. At ten he had become a vegetarian, so as not to do harm to any.

Nevertheless, granted that I had tried to bring him up with a spirit of generosity, this open-jar policy was carrying things too far! I must hurry back inside the cottage to tidy the kitchen—after lecturing him, of course, on the proper place for jar tops and for ants. Like the stars overhead, they should learn where they belong.

Then I remembered the broiling January afternoon in Malaysia, when Alexander emerged from the jungle path between the coconut palms, a plastic bag tied to his fat-tired bike.

"I brought you a present," he announced. I looked forward to an exotic plant, perhaps a wild white orchid, or some peculiar fruit.

He parked his bike under the banyan tree and loosed the neck of the bag.

"His name is Henry," he said. A delicate snake of brilliant jade green emerged from the bag.

Henry started circling Alexander's arm, spiraling up around his neck.

"Shouldn't he have a more Malay name?" I asked, watching the slender and friendly green snake. "At least something like *Si Ular*." In old Malay folk tales, the clever, even too clever, animals sometimes sported the prefix *Si*. "Si Ular" would be something like Sir Snake.

We were accustomed to our safe American blacksnakes, and knew that many of the snakes out here were as harmless: of course there were the cobras and kraits. Henry, slender and green, was certainly neither.

As I stood watching Henry, or Si Henry Ular, weave around Alexander's head, suddenly I remembered where I had seen such a snake. In the Washington Zoo.

Yes, it was a Southeast Asian snake all right: the Malayan Pit-Viper.

Henry's head immediately took on highly triangular dimensions.

"You know, Alexander," I began quietly, "that lovely little snake should really be returned to his jungle now. . . . Do put him back in the bag. . . . Immediately. . . . They get nervous with too much man-handling."

"*Snake*-handling," Alexander corrected me. He blew softly on the back of that leathery head. "Henry really is very calm. Just active now because it's a hot day. I'm thirsty. I'll get him some water too." They went into the house. I heard the sound of the pitcher of boiled water pouring into a glass.

"Yes, dear, but then do put him back . . . in the bag . . . and then to the jungle, back where you found him. Ver-r-ry carefully."

From the doorway I watched Henry gently circle Alexander's arms and hands, flick his tongue against the

53

moist sides of the glass. The hens were crowding into the doorway, hoping for corn. I worried they would startle the snake. Just as Alexander might jump suddenly and scare it if I were too hasty in warning him what he actually had in hand.

But perhaps animals sense gentleness, fearlessness, love.

At last Henry slid down Alexander's arm into the waiting bag.

"That happens to be a highly poisonous Malayan Pit-Viper," I said when the bag was finally closed.

"Okay, okay, so I'll put him back," Alexander was unperturbed. Perhaps he had suspected the risk all along? He disappeared down into the swamp, bag bulging, returning with it empty.

"But you were supposed to take him far away—not just to our swamp!"

Little thicker than a millipede, Henry could slither inside anytime. Mentally I nailed weatherstripping to the bottom of the door. In reality, as with many of my realities, I never got around to it. Who would have weatherstripping materials in Southeast Asia anyway?

Nor did it prove necessary. Henry knew his place.

Now the visiting scientist was edging down the splintery dock in the starlit Maryland dark. He lectured us that here in the northern hemisphere again, we had entered astronomical autumn. And it was mighty chilly out there now. And when would supper be ready?

"After the ants have finished their dinner," Alexander muttered in Malay.

"I've cleaned up the kitchen," the scientist proclaimed in English.

Electric lights dazzled us after the stars. But I could still see a few ants at the fringes of kitchen.

"Do you know you have mice?" demanded our friend.

I followed his look.

"Mice? Oh, so we do!"

An autumnal field mouse. The seasons were changing: time to move inside.

Dashing like a shadow on toothpick legs, the mouse kept his ears—like pink lettuce—alert. He seemed not to fear us: his was only a reconnaissance mission. But the floor had been swept.

"We must put out some cheese," said Alexander. 🐀

'Hour Dogging' In Montana
Hallett Stromholt

We called them "hour dogs" because they woke the camp up in the dark to get out on the line before anyone else and get the jump on time and wages planting trees. 🐾 How many mornings had I thought of the proverb, he who blesses "with a loud voice, rising early in the morning, it shall be counted a curse to him." 🐾

As I lay in my sleeping bag, feeling as though I'd been hit by a truck the day before from the rigors of planting trees in the rock and rough country of high mountains, *they* snapped branches for kindling, rattled pots and pans, laughed, and one actually *sang.*

Their noise signified that we (they called us "the late crew") had less than an hour to get up, be out on the line by 6:45 a.m., swinging the heavy hoedads into hard soil, roots, subsurface rock, to make a deep hole where a fresh tree might have a chance where loggers 20 years ago had cleaned out everything.

It was our valley's forte, this tree planting, and every spring we fanned out from the Huerfano in Colorado to wherever our computers had won us a bid with the Forest Service. It was one of the things many of us did for our home and children, besides the jobs we invented, our cottage industries, for there is little formal employment in our area. It was on the job in Montana that I found out about "hour dogging."

We good-humoredly let the "hour dogs" do it. After all, we had 150,000 trees to plant, and the sooner done, the sooner home. But they were annoying, our own people, coming in in the evening with 12 hours to record in the book to our humble "10s."

And what's more, they had their own clubby humor. All day long they'd yell back and forth "I'm *in*!" Meaning: They had just planted a tree at the required depth, no J-roots, no rocks, an 18-inch scalp around the tree, which wasn't easy. To the late crew, even midmorning or after lunch they'd say, "You in, yet?" even though you'd planted hundreds. And at lunch they seemed relaxed, in *bonne forme,* talking as at a picnic, while we'd eat and faze out for a snooze.

One day toward the end of the contract, after hot weather, when you had to sleep out of your bag for the sunburn on arms and shoulders, I decided to get up early and work in the cool, get my "10," and quit in the afternoon. It was an effort. But once I had "crossed over" from the soft sleeping to upright on the hard ground outside my tent, I was surprised how painless it was.

Something cool in the lightening air invigorated my lungs, challenged my memory with—what was it? thoughts of youth fishing at a lake with my father . . . ? or was it the smell of hay and manure and the light dew at the farm?

I was really awake to something. It was beautiful silky air. I made my tea and honey, swallowed presoaked granola, grabbed my hoedad, gloves, tree bag, harness, and walked down the road to the gulley we were planting.

Seven of the early crew were already lined up, hoedads flashing in the first rays of sun down on the Montana plain. They were quiet. I was surprised. There were no catcalls when they saw me. One of them said, "Did you see that fawn down by the tree, Hal?" I went down to look. There it was. On the way back up to the line I saw a turkey creep off into the brush.

I settled in and began swinging. It didn't hurt as much as I thought, the jarring, without that hour's sleep. One, the one who sings, I saw his lips moving in meditation ever so slightly; was he praying during this hour? I spotted a hawk coming into its nest from the night, carrying something.

I worried about the fawn for a while as I worked, then turning to reach a tree from my bag saw its mother in the lightened tree line below. I got warmed up, in a bold and relaxed rhythm of work. The morning air had given me something to think about. I had hidden treasure for the whole day.

My thoughts were pierced, not by the screaming of a hawk, but something similar. "Hey, Robo! You *in* yet?" It was the earliest of the "late crew" coming now to work with us, getting a friendly heckle by the singer. Now I saw what the "hour doggers" were defending: How could anyone have slept through the hour that had just passed? Why, it would take them the whole day to catch up with us. 🐗

THE CAT WHO ATE SPAGHETTI, THE DOG WHO CHASED COWS
Guernsey LePelley

Some people like cats more than dogs. I don't commit myself either way, because this issue can burn with more prejudice than when a Democrat turns up at a Republican family picnic.

There are distinct differences between dogs and cats and consequently differences between dog owners and cat owners. So if one said he didn't like cats, it's almost the same as saying he didn't like people who like cats. However, it doesn't work quite the same in reverse. One can say he doesn't like dogs and nobody cares. I suspect cats know this, which accounts for their somewhat superior attitude.

There was a time in our family's less disciplined days when we had two smallish children, two medium-sized cats, and two dogs of varied size. One dog was a terrier and the other an Irish setter. The cats were named Topsy and Saucy, the terrier's name was Skipper, and the setter was Daniel of Killarney.

Looking back on it now, I guess the animals were better trained than the children. Anyway, the children were required to eat their meals off dinner plates at the dining room table, while the animals were forbidden to do so. They weren't even allowed in the dining room during mealtime. In strict obedience to the letter of the law, cats and dogs would line up in the kitchen doorway about a quarter inch from forbidden territory, which meant that anyone attempting to go from kitchen to dining room would have to step over a formidable line of patient animals.

Dinner guests were amazed at such perfect behavior. Once when a guest commented on the well-behaved menagerie, my wife said, "Oh, Kin [that's what I am called] trained them not to bother us at mealtime." Whereupon, filled with modesty, I added, "They won't come in until I tell them it's OK." Of course at the word OK, bedlam was released and cats and dogs bounded into the dining room like the Red Sea falling in on the Egyptians.

There is something I must add to this. While generally the animals were respectfully obedient, about twice a month without warning, Saucy the cat would suddenly streak through the dining room into the living room to hide under the sofa. The next day, however, Saucy would take her place at the kitchen door as if nothing had happened.

Cats are either overestimated or underestimated when it comes to intelligence. Either they are dumb, or they are smart enough to pretend they are dumb. For instance, when the dogs wanted to come into the house they generally went to what was called the river door, which led into the living room. When they barked briefly for admittance I would say, "Go to the kitchen door." They would then promptly circle the house to the kitchen side.

But not the cats! The cats would stand in what appeared to be a sort of mental fog until the world came to an end, or until friend wife would come mop them with a towel.

The dogs and cats were respectful of each other. The cats knew they belonged, and although terrified of other dogs, they sought safety in the genial tolerance of Skipper and Danny. Topsy would even curl up next to the warmth of Danny's soft, red coat and Danny, embarrassed, would reluctantly allow it.

Danny was the same with crawling babies, who in play would often hit him too hard. Topsy and Saucy were not so trustworthy.

The animals were considerate of each other's food dishes and were fairly neat eaters. The exceptions were when the dogs had a bone, they had to take it out to the backyard and not wrestle with it on the kitchen floor.

In the case of Saucy the cat, she had a rather vulgar way of eating spaghetti that held the whole family spellbound. She would suck the long strands into her mouth one at a time so that the very end would slap around before disappearing, leaving the nose and face covered with meat sauce. It was a better performance than Morris ever did with 9 Lives.

Habits varied with the different animals. When Danny was very young he had an impulse to chase cows. Neither the farmers nor the cows saw the fun in this that Danny did, so Danny had to be quickly trained to respect a cow's indolent chewing. If temptation ever seemed about to overpower him, it was enough to say, "Danny, don't chase the cows." Cows weren't bothered by the cats. The closest they ever came to a cow was a saucer of milk.

So, cow-chasing as a sport came to an end. One morning, however, I looked out the window and Danny was chasing a deer at the upper end of the property. No one had the foresight to include deer in the list of unchasable items, so I didn't know what to do. On impulse I went out on the porch and shouted, "Danny, don't chase the cows."

Well, Danny stopped, but I never saw a more indignant dog. He knew the difference between a cow and a deer but evidently people didn't. I tried explaining it to Danny, but I had the feeling I had failed an IQ test.

Afternoons, Danny and Skipper would hear the school bus coming far in the distance and would race to the stopping place to greet No. 2 son with joyful leaps and barks. Neither Topsy nor Saucy knew a school bus from a garbage truck, but they would dutifully rub an ankle once the child was in the house.

Whenever I had problems to solve I would go out beside the rushing river just to think. The cats understood meditation but Danny didn't. Anyone standing silently was too much for Danny. He would circle around me, trying to detect the game, then would start barking furiously for me to wake up. Because of this it has always been difficult for anyone in our family to sit silently without someone's barking at him.

Some people prefer cats to dogs. Some prefer dogs to cats. And some people just prefer people. In our case, when people, dogs, cats, and children gathered together of an evening, there were no favorites. ❧

ALICE AND THE YELLOW LEAVES
Dennis Mayes

On one of those stimulating autumn days that teases you with the notion that had you rushed outside at sunrise you could have glimpsed the wizard who annually refurbishes the sky with a brush dipped in Pacific blue, I stood on the front lawn, hands folded over a rake, contemplating leaves. ❧

I do not know how long I stood there, nor how long I was observed, before a young voice said, "You're not going to rake the yellow ones, are you?"

A little girl with one foot on the curb, the other on a pedal of her bicycle, had asked. I frequently saw her pumping past my house late in the afternoon. I knew she lived around the corner but until that day our acquaintance was limited to smiles and waves. Her name, she said, was Alice.

It was the tallest tree in the yard, dropping its leaves in a bright yellow circle around its trunk, that occasioned our introduction. "I don't know, Alice. Shouldn't I rake them?"

"I wouldn't," she said. The positive tone of this remark suggested she had given the mounding yellow her most serious consideration. "You know why those leaves are more yellow than the others, don't you?"

Experience has taught me to approach such a question from an eight-year-old with a degree of caution. While I was trying to determine whether I should include in my answer such terms as "chlorophyll" or "photo-synthesis"—or merely concede at the outset, "No, why?"—Alice volunteered her theory.

"They've been on the tree all summer, see, and since that is the tallest tree, it soaked up the most sunshine."

I believe my response was slightly less profound, something like, "Um . . . well . . . ." Perhaps logic of such crystalline purity momentarily stunned me. I do remember stammering, "So, if I leave them . . . leave leaves . . . ?"

Alice, putting hand on hip, regarded me as if unable to comprehend how anyone of my vintage could have progressed so far in life with a mind so dense. "In winter the sun stays behind the clouds more, so where do you think a tree gets its sunshine?"

"I see! From these leaves! They break down over time, melt away like ice cubes, and their sunshine seeps down to the tree roots?"

Apparently I caught on quickly enough to redeem myself, because Alice laid down her bike and we sat beside the circle of radiance, she to continue my education, I to marvel at the Wonderland of her imagination.

"That's how I figure it must work," said Alice. "I bet if you let the leaves stay, the grass will be greener there next year." It was an experiment I could not refuse.

One early evening the following May, Alice wheeled her bike onto my driveway to inquire if I would sponsor her, at a nickel a lap, in her swim team's charity meet. As I signed my pledge I said, "Have you noticed? The grass where we left the sunshine piled up is not only greener, the blades are a half-inch taller than anywhere else in the lawn." Alice was too polite to mention she told me so.

I saw Alice in June when she came to collect for her *stellar* performance at the swim meet, but not again for three months. I was setting out chrysanthemums in a flower bed. A breeze persuaded the tall tree to sprinkle me with the first drops of what would become this year's shower of sunshine. It seemed to blow Alice along from nowhere, atop a pair of all-terrain roller skates. She regarded me from curbside, unaccountably shy, looking somewhat older and wiser and sadly embarrassed when I asked about her summer.

Finally, she blurted, "Guess you think I'm really dumb." Her tone, suggesting a recent upheaval in self-confidence, signaled that the time had come to forget chrysanthemums and amble curbside for a heart-to-heart chat. Alice's newfound uncertainty derived in part from her experience at a summer camp, where she "majored in science."

"Miss La Berra helped me with my project. She teaches botany, and she said I was wrong about your tree and the grass. It isn't sunshine. It's only a natural cycle. The tree takes food out of the ground and puts it in the leaves, somehow, then the leaves get full and turn yellow and fall off and rot and feed new leaves next year. Composting is what you're supposed to call it. Someone old as you probably knew all along, didn't you? I sure was wrong."

61

"Alice," I confessed, "I knew. But you know something else? In a way, you are as right as Miss Botanist."

After Alice skated homeward, I did something really dumb for someone as old as I, something really wonderful . . . sprawled on my back in the grass and gazed up at the tall tree.

Had Alice understood what I said about the possibility of there being a single truth, expressed differently through the visions of poets and scientists? Through the years, as she looks at things from the myriad perspectives awaiting her discovery, will she remember this yard, this tree, and me with embarrassment?

I prefer to think that one fine autumn day when Alice finds herself in my state of advancing antiquity, an eight-year-old will pop up from nowhere, enabling her to rekindle the wonderment of childhood, to forget what neighbors might think, to sprawl in her front lawn and study a drop of sunshine twirling, spiraling, fluttering toward her like an unexpected blessing from a sky of ocean blue.

As that sparkle of remembrance descends, brushes past upraised hand, I know she, too, will be startled by joy as she discovers that one never grows too old, too informed, to reach out and be touched by the marvel of life renewing itself.

South Dakota Night
Linda M. Hasselstrom

At midnight in midwinter the sky is a deep blue-black, lit only by a few cold stars and shards of ice in the deepest ruts. 🐚 The temperature reached nearly fifty today, and the scent from the deep golden grasses on the rolling hills south of the house hangs in the air, tangy and sweet, mixed with the sharper odor of manure from the corrals, and the heavy scent of burning wood. 🐚 Moonlight gives a faint silver sheen to tall bronze bluestem, tawny foxtail, brown alfalfa. 🐚

I turn slowly, enjoying a skyline shaped by the smooth shapes of hills; no straight-sided buildings break that gently arch, no trees slash upward. This is the prairie, during the annual warm spell between the first snow and the spring storms that strike when our cows begin calving in March. To the north, a glow marks the nearest town, twenty miles away. If I lean forward over the porch railing, I can see my neighbor's yard light a mile away.

As a city child, I lived in terror of the dark. Even now, on brief city visits, I lock doors and look wistfully out high windows at night, awakened by sirens and inexplicable shrieks. Out here, where strange sounds in the night may mean a prairie fire or someone stealing cows, I can't avoid the responsibility of investigating. But here the night is more than peaceful; it is inviting, an opportunity not to be missed. Often, I get up and prowl outside in my night-gown just for the pleasure of it.

On a moonless night when I was a teen-ager, I found myself on a tired horse far from home after dark. Coyotes howled; a booming rush overhead told me the nighhawks were hunting insects. In my fear, I complained to my horse, who blew her warm breath on my face and reminded me a good horse

63

will take a rider home even in a blizzard. I mounted, loosened the reins, and waited. She raised her head and began trotting confidently straight into smothering blackness, as if a sack had dropped over my head. But I trusted her. Soon the nighthawks swirling around me became benevolent night spirits; the coyotes sounded happy to be alive. Grass swished against my horse's legs just as it did in daylight; my saddle squeaked. After awhile, I could see the birds, and the grass seemed to glow faintly, as if lit from within. Before I'd seen enough, I was home. My fear was gone.

A coyote howls from the east, near the carcass of a cow that died of old age yesterday. In the distance a series of puppy-like yips and yaps begin, and I can trace the young coyotes' high-spirited progress through the gully toward the dead cow by their cheerful arguing. If I wanted to leave the porch and walk a half-mile to the hilltop, I could hear them growling over the old cow's thin ribs. The cow had borne calves for us for almost twenty years, until her hips grated and rattled from the strain of her age. We thanked her as we dragged her to the pile of ancestral bones.

Directly below me, tall weeds around a waterhole rattle briefly—a coyote hunting mice, or a skunk headed for the compost, or the seven deer come for water. A yearling calf bawls, one of the bunch of twenty-six heifers we're raising for replacement breeding cows. They've been fed together since they were weaned and always move—like teenagers—in a compact and usually raucous bunch. Faintly I can see black shapes lying close together a half-mile away, and a light-colored blotch moving toward them from a gully. Perhaps they left her while she napped, and she woke alone, frightened as a child.

I inhale deeply, glad the blizzard roared over our heads two days ago. We could almost inhale snow from the heavy gray clouds, and the winds left a fifteen-foot hole in the plank corral, plastic flapping on barbed wire, hamburger cartons jammed under tumbleweeds in fence corners. The next blizzard is on its way, and we may not get off so lightly next time. When snow is piled deep on the plains, so even normal sounds are muffled, I put on my sheepskin moccasins before my midnight trips. But I still go.

If I'm patient, on some night when the thermometer reads ten or fifteen degrees below zero, I will hear the grouse calling. First a single note, like the mellow tone of a monastery bell, will ring form the top of a haystack, and be answered from the shelter of the willows down the gully. I'll try to get outside without making a sound. If I shut a door too hard, or speak, or even shiver, they stop and may not start again that night.

But if I am quiet enough, I might listen to them ringing back and forth across the prairie for an hour. Finally, with a thoroughly undignified squawk, the first one will launch itself awkwardly and fly toward the others. Then they will all take off, floundering in the air like flying turtles, clucking and muttering, until they bury themselves under a rosebush to peck after seeds and gossip for the rest of the night.

Then I move, take a step and hear the snow squeal with cold underfoot. Each step seems to reverberate until I can hear nothing else. The world shrinks to the sound of my footsteps—painfully symbolic—until I stop, and wait for the natural sounds to reassert themselves.

The neighbor's dog barks, a high, frantic yelping. The spell of the moonlight is broken. I'll come back another night, after the snow, to hear the grouse. Now it's time to go back to bed, the warm tangle of husband, dog and cat, to drift back to sleep among faint coyote howls. ⟩

From Small Beginnings
Ruskin Bond

On the first clear day of September, towards the end of the rains, I visited the pine knoll, my place of peace and power. 🐚

It was months since I'd last been there. Trips to the plains, a crisis in my affairs, involvements with other people and their troubles, and an entire monsoon, had come between me and the grassy, pine-topped slope facing the eternal snows of the Himalayas. Now I tramped through late monsoon foliage—tall ferns, wild balsam, bushes festooned with flowering convolvulus—crossed the stream by way of the little bridge of stones, and climbed the steep hill to the pine slope.

When the trees saw me they made as if to turn in my direction. A puff of wind came across the valley from the distant snows. A long tailed blue magpie took alarm and flew noisily out of an oak tree. The cicadas were suddenly silent. But the trees remembered me. They bowed in the breeze and beckoned me nearer, welcoming me home—three pines, a straggling oak, and a wild cherry. I went among them, acknowledged their welcome with a touch of my hand against their trunks, the cherry's smooth and polished; the pine's patterned and whorled; the oak's rough, gnarled, full of experience. He's been there the longest, and the wind had bent his upper branches and twisted a few, so that he looked shaggy and undistinguished. But, like the philosopher who is careless about his dress and appearance, the oak has secrets, a hidden wisdom. He has learned the art of survival.

While the oak and the pines are older than I, and have been here many years, the cherry tree is exactly ten years old. I know, because I planted it.

One day I had a cherry seed in my hand and on an impulse, I thrust it into the soft earth and then went away and forgot all about it. A few months later I found a tiny cherry tree in the long grass. I did not expect it to survive. But the following year it was two feet tall. And then some goats ate the young leaves, and a grasscutter's scythe injured the stem, and I was sure the tree would wither away. But it renewed itself, sprang up even faster, and within three years was a healthy growing tree, about five feet tall.

I left the hills for a few years—forced by circumstances to make a living in the plains—but this time I did not forget the cherry tree. I thought about it quite often, sending it messages of love and encouragement. And when, last year, I returned in the autumn, my heart did a somersault when I found my tree sprinkled with pale pink blossoms. (The Himalayan cherry flowers in November.) Later, when the fruit was ripe, the tree visited by finches, tits, bulbuls, and other small birds, all coming to feast on the sour red cherries.

Last summer I spent a night on the pine knoll, sleeping on the grass beneath the cherry tree. I lay awake for hours, listening to the chatter of the stream and the occasional tonk-tonk of a nightjar, and watching, through the branches overhead, at the stars turning in the sky, and I felt the power of sky and earth, and the power of a small cherry seed.

And so, when the rains are over, this is where I come, that I may feel the peace and power of this magic place. It's a big world, and momentous events are taking place all the time. But this is where I have seen it happen. 🐚

'CAN I KEEP IT?'
Eleanor Weston

'Mom! Mart! Look! Can I keep it?" ❧ The Kid galloped toward me dangling what I thought for sure must be a boa constrictor. ❧ "I found it in the field," he cried breathlessly. ❧

The other boys gathered round, while the owner of the field paused mid-sentence to say, "Fine little red racer ya got yourself there, young fella. Makes a dandy little pet." The scream that had been gathering momentum got stuck in my throat. Little? Pet? Red racer?

"Well, Mom, can I?"

"Can you what?"

"Can I keep him?"

The field we were in was filled with a glory of late summer daisies, Queen Anne's lace, purple thistles, and brown fuzzies that stick to socks. In addition, there were bedsprings, a few sinks, and several huge tires. The field was owned by a grizzled man of indeterminate age in overalls and no shirt. And in fact, it wasn't a field at all but his backyard. He had an old Harley-Davidson motorcycle for sale, and The Old Man and I and various of our boys had driven some 65 miles from my home in the concrete jungle of Seattle to his home in the foothills of the Cascades to see this Harley. And maybe even buy it.

"That snake," I began, eyeing it from a distance, "deserves to be in that field . . . ('that's not a field, ma'am, that's my yard') . . . in that yard, free to roam with his family, free to catch rodents, free to . . . ('the cats catch the rodents, ma'am, and sometimes even the snakes') . . . ." The Kid was shocked.

"You're going to force me to abandon my snake to some killer cat?" he shouted. "Besides," he added, lowering his voice, perhaps suspecting that country folk might not take kindly to city kids yelling at their moms, "snakes may deserve to be in fields, but a boy deserves to have a snake."

I was astounded by my momentary lapse. How could I have forgotten what a boy deserves! We ended up with a free snake instead of a Harley and drove home with one boy lovingly clutching a jar with a snake inside and three other boys wishing it was theirs.

We got home and The Kid enthusiastically set up the aquarium: a jar lid of water, some apple slices, a couple of hamburger curds, and gravel from the neighbor's Japanese garden. My boys went to a birthday party across the street; the Old Man and his boys went home; and I went out to dinner. When I came back, I called the birthday party mom, asked her about the party, told her she could send the boys home anytime she liked, and as an afterthought asked if she had heard about our latest pet.

"Well, yes," she said, "it's just hard to imagine how it escaped."

"Escaped?" My throat went dry. My life flashed before me.

It seems that the birthday party had diligently trooped over to see the snake and it was gone when they got there. I tore the house apart and indeed the snake had vanished. I spent the next few nights sleeping fretfully, assuming that the snake would slither his way into the bedroom and join me in the cozy confines of my bed. I spent the next few days trying to buy a mongoose.

That was six years ago. Since then we've had other pets, and we seem to have a particular affinity for escape artists or critters with eating habits which I alone seem able to fulfill.

We got mice at the pet store. I was suspicious from the beginning. I was assured, however, by the enthusiastic pet store lady and My Two Sons that, indeed, they were pet mice, not real mice. Well, I finally agreed, they were cute: transparent ears, permanently moving noses, tiny wavering whiskers, and alert black dots for eyes. Of course we had to buy four: One would be lonesome, so get two. Whose room would they sleep in? Simple enough, get two for each room.

We found that pet mice turn into real mice when they escape, which they do as easily as Houdini. In a few days they were all over the place. And just like real mice, they scampered around, hid behind the refrigerator, and reappeared only in the middle of the night when I was alone and reading or during dinner parties. Furthermore, they lured the cats—obtained in grocery store parking lots—into peculiar behavior. Such as rousing themselves from a sleep-a-thon in *my* armchair, walking to the front door, and begging to be let out on a dark and stormy night. Anything rather than committing such catlike acts as catching a mouse. Particularly a recycled pet mouse.

We got our chameleon at the State Fair. He lived in an aquarium (more garage sales) on the radiator in the kitchen. He walked up the twig and turned brown; he walked down the twig into the gravel (yes, the neighbor's Japanese garden again) and turned gray. He ate spiders hand-caught by yours truly, who discovered that the Munchkin is afraid of spiders and The Kid is missing when it is time to replenish the arachnid supply.

One day someone told me that chameleons like to eat crickets, so off I went, logically, to the fish store. There I was told that crickets are sold in three sizes and that chameleons prefer small crickets which are available on Tuesdays, and wasn't I lucky, it was Monday and I could simply come back tomorrow. The next day, Tuesday, small-cricket day, I bought 25 small crickets for 50 cents. The happy chameleon immediately downed two and then ignored the other 23, which all escaped and then lived in unfindable places in the house. For the next few weeks our house was like a camping trip: silence all day and crickets chirping all night.

I chose to buy only three or four crickets at a time after that, always small ones on Tuesday and always wondering if Monday's crickets weren't perhaps last Tuesday's crickets all grown up. When the fish store salesperson tried to talk me into buying fish, I told her that all our aquariums were being used. One for the cricket-eating chameleon and one for the guaranteed male teddy bear hamster and its four babies.

It did occur to me, however, that perhaps I could keep a bowl full of water on the mantelpiece and tell the kids it was full of guppies that were too small to see. ◥

THE NATURE OF THINGS

Freedom, And Lessons In Fortitude
Henrietta Buckmaster

"History" is one of those convenience words without any real meaning. ❧ It can arrange to be all things to all people. ❧ Its convenience is measured by its availability in emergencies or emotional crises. ❧ It may have academic usefulness, but that seems to be subordinate to its willingness to surprise. ❧

As a child I loved it. It explained cathedrals and controversies to me, paintings and points of view. It was the only subject in which I got unbroken 100s. I was very selective about the dates I remembered because I had satisfied myself, early on, that dates and facts had very little to do with what really happened.

History's only purpose, it seemed to me, was to give perspective and comfort. *Look at what mankind has survived!* I could say. *Look at our innate good sense and perspicacity! Look at how evil rose AND fell.* The principal lesson, I believe, was to get the eyes open so that one might be skeptical of assumptions, view stereotypes with astonishment, and take heart.

It's time that I say this essay is not about history. But it is about one very important person's experience which changed my life. Its impetus came from a nagging conviction that history might have different information about some of the fantasies and ambiguities that were grouped under "conventional wisdom" and written down by historians.

I was young enough to think that any relation between "conventional" and "wisdom" must be a solecism. What made me question it most were the black people.

I was white. I never saw any blacks except the very nice colored woman who came to clean once a week, or the porter who carried my mother's bags as we went back and forth to the country. There were none in my school, none in the congregation of our church, none on the outskirts of my parents' friends, none in our apartment house—except the janitor's assistant—none in the movies I saw except the chronic lazy-good-for-nothing. I wondered why and got ambiguous answers. Our cleaning woman was treated with the utmost kindness and given the things we didn't need. There was no ill will, just a great deal of abysmal darkness on all sides.

When I took my questions outside my family, I did not like any of the suggestions offered, such as: Blacks were blacks, an inferior people. It wasn't their fault, but we'd only make it harder if we pretended otherwise. They had been brought here from the Dark Continent (which had no history) and held in slavery (which automatically made a nonperson). As for slavery, it received two paragraphs in my history book and was brought to an end by Abraham Lincoln.

Slavery was very unfortunate, my teacher agreed; it shouldn't have happened, but if anyone had to be enslaved—and even Thomas Jefferson held slaves—it was better that it be a people with no background, no memory, no culture, and brought to a country where at least they learned English.

It's funny how these things affect one. It sounded as though a race had been collectively aborted. If history had so little common sense, I needed to reexamine our friendship with her.

Yet the uses and abuses of history were no surprise; since I had read around and through it from the age of ten and knew with my intuition that people made of it what they wanted and concealed what was awkward. This had seemed a grown-up ploy, but now I was eighteen—grown up—and chose to see this as a moral issue. I began to separate history from historians. I began to make remarkable discoveries. I began to find what I was searching for.

During the summer of that year I spent each evening in library files. It was a pleasure being obliged to do what you liked doing. It was a pleasure to see a people and a culture begin to take shape. It was all there, documented but ignored—the great empires of Africa when the Europeans were forest dwellers, the great centers of learning from Timbuktu to Zanzibar before the universities of Italy, France and England were more than a dream. The first black men brought forcibly to America came as indentured servants, not slaves; one was already so admirably educated that he won his independence and a place on the faculty of Cambridge University in England.

Slavery, marked for extermination by the Founding Fathers, had a burst of new life when cotton acquired a technology, the cotton gin, which separated cotton fiber from seeds faster than any human hands. Cotton became the

73

economic system of the South and determined the mores of the 19th century. Ten times more slaves were needed—twenty times more—to maintain the incredible prosperity, and the terrible slave-bearing ships beat through the waves of the Atlantic and slave breeding farms were set up in Virginia. Fortunes were made. It was said that the investment in slavery came to represent the combined worth of the four largest industries in the United States. Certainly it dominated the political, social, religious and economic life of the country.

The most interesting detail I found was that slaves did not all sing at their work, as the historians implied. Nor that the South was modeled after *Gone With the Wind.* There was such a thing as the "underground railroad," and it had taken shape in the minds of the slaves who rode its invisible rails into freedom. Two took the "railroad" nailed into crates, some took it by clinging to the sides of coast steamers. Most spoke with their feet, following the North Star and trusting desperately to the ingenuity of the "station keepers," whites and free blacks who hated slavery. It was always a perilous business. There was no easy way to make the long journey from Mississippi across the Mason-Dixon line, or the short journey from Maryland, since no part of the law was on your side. After the Fugitive Slave Law of 1850, the journey was not complete until you reached Canada, and the penalties for those who helped could be total bankruptcy and even, in some cases, their lives. One day in that year 60,000 people lined the streets of Boston to cry "shame!" when a runaway Virginia slave named Burns was returned by government steamer to his master, an act that was only accomplished by a battalion of Light Dragoons, 22 companies of artillery and infantry, a company of marines and the cost of $40,000. "A few more such victories and the South is undone," the Richmond, Virginia, *Enquirer,* observed.

I had heard a little about the underground railroad because train after train had run through Ohio to Lake Erie, and Ohio was the land of my forebears. What I had not heard about—what was by no means common knowledge—were the slave uprisings, over 200 in the hundred years before the Civil War, three massive ones, two in Virginia, led by Nat Turner and by Gabriel, one in South Carolina, led by Denmark Vesey. They were famous in their time, shaking the slavocracy, and leading to even more stringent laws.

And I knew nothing about the ex-slaves who became newspaper publishers, lecturers, diplomats, doctors, ministers and, after the Civil War, US senators (two) and US representatives (five).

One evening the librarian (of this library in Harlem where I spent my evenings) sat down at my desk. She had been calling up and delivering to me the array of information that was affecting my life. She whispered, "Will you tell me why you are asking for these things?" I told her I was writing a book from the point of view of what really happened. She whispered, "I hope you know how important it is," and then, still whispering, she said, "Our children think they have no background. Their history books teach them they came from nowhere. Let them know something else."

Black children don't think that anymore. Many white people don't think that anymore. It's not that human backgrounds count for so much—they're badly flawed in any case—but the truth counts. To be told you're nothing and have only obscure evidence to disprove this takes an intestinal fortitude that no one has the right to demand.

Demanding this of yourself is another matter. That's why I especially love my black friends. They knew what they had to do. They knew they had to make the evidence out of their own lives. They taught me what fortitude means. It's a debt that takes a long time to repay. ᕕ

ON HUMOR
Neil Millar

They resembled picture-book angels on Jacob's ladder, and they were laughing. ෨

Now where did that little vision come from?

I was listening for a lead into this serious essay on humor, when these lovely guests arrived at the gate of my attention. I mention them now, not as a contribution to space fiction or angelology, but simply as a personal imagining of radiant fellow-travelers. Who were they? Visitors from a distant galaxy? That is not clear to me, but this is: they were laughing because they were enjoying the human condition—from the outside.

And who wouldn't enjoy it, from the outside? Mankind may well be the greatest joke in the universe.

How do *we* see this joke? That depends, I think, not only on our sense of humor, but also on our sense of love and our sense of magic. Without those three, working together, we'll never see our world. (By "magic" I just mean divinity perceptible in action; signs of it are everywhere, even in affectionate jokes.)

He who stands on his dignity will certainly fall off—and will be laughed at. He who enjoys laughing at himself will never lack reason for merriment. To be human is to be funny. Mankind is a collective jest so comical that we're not at all likely to be attacked by visitors from outer space, even if the visitors aren't angelic. (If they know about us at all, they'll be friendly because we're funny. Who would wage war on a four-billion-ring circus, the Greatest Show in Space?)

Humanity, as many sages have observed, takes itself far too solemnly. This is a grave mistake: without humor's clear-eyed affection, earnestness can degenerate into bigotry and fanaticism; and these blind shadows consider themselves light.

In the corridors of power, humor is vital. Even when it's clumsy, it does what agile wit cannot. And the clown isn't always clumsy: he can be as nimble as a squirrel.

The best wit is cool, and makes startling common sense. The best humor, being warm, is a kind of wild poetry that makes mincemeat of common sense. Wit must be elegant; humor need not be so. Pomposity and wit seldom go together: the latter destroys the former; but humor delights in pomposity and would never destroy it.

What of the humble pun, that "lowest form of wit," that catalyst of humor? Here's an example from history: Sir Robert Walpole, a man of peace, had led England through many tranquil years. When he was forced to declare war (in 1739) his country celebrated the catastrophe as if it were glory: the chimes hung clamoring in the pearly London sky. "They now ring their bells," said Walpole, "but they will soon wring their hands."

That sad little observation was wit. It was also black humor—the dark, defeated grin that lends itself too easily to pain. Black humor goes down fighting; but humor of any other color stays up fighting. If cornered, it retaliates with an inspired irrelevance that robs defeat of submission.

It cuts trouble down to manageable size. Perhaps that's why the Great Depression of the 1930s was also a great age of American comedians: they were needed then, and everyone knew it. They are still needed, but who knows it?

Few serious fiction writers seem to. In today's padded prosperity, literature often appears to celebrate misery above joy, and black humor above all other kinds. Why? Do readers need vicarious unhappiness to expiate the fashionable vicarious guilt? I don't believe in this guilt; but even if I did, I would see no merit in unhappiness, vicarious or otherwise.

But what if the reading public *prefers* misery to humor? Well, I'm a member of the reading public, and *I* prefer humor. Grief is my ancient enemy, and gray tales only strengthen him. I have fought this adversary since childhood, and expect to go on fighting him—with jokes. Some of the jokes have been pretty feeble; they could hardly hobble into battle; yet misery trembled before them.

It seems to me that much literary grayness results from an unconscious intellectual black joke: the notion that sensitive people are so horrified by the world's despair that they dutifully add to it. Couldn't they be equally sensitive to the world's happiness, and add to that instead?

The world's happiness. Why are we here, in this human condition, on

77

this lovely little planet? I can't believe we've come to learn misery's wizened arts; joy is the norm in the panoramas of light. Have we come to learn laughter, then? This seems highly probable to me. Could there be, anywhere in our endless journey, a likelier laughter-school than Earth?

Even, perhaps, for visitors from outer space? ❦

Night Landings
Tom Simmons

We're on final approach to San Francisco. It's been a long flight through bad weather; the rain drives down hard through the darkness. The flight attendants have turned down the cabin lights. Below us is water—the still-invisible currents and whitecaps of the San Francisco Bay.

Pilots know that following a westerly compass heading along the bay will take them directly to runways 28L and 28R. Passengers, who are not obliged to think about such things, have more time to spend with the scene itself—the descent into darkness, on extended wings.

Landing over water at night is completely different from landing over land. Coming in over land, over suburbs and industrial parks, the plane finds an incandescent welcome mat.

Over water this comforting familiarity disappears. It's out there, of course: we can see the distant lights. But what is below us? Nothing—nothing but water, darkness. This might seem ominous, but for me the opposite is true. Landing over water offers a different order of comfort. These landings reenact one of my favorite modern dances, in which the partners are nature and machine. In an unchoreographed waltz, each partner leads, and each follows, and neither is the master—or both are; until finally, skidding synthetic rubber on concrete, the airplane returns to the human world and leaves its dark partner behind.

What are the steps to this improvised dance? On the machine's side, they are almost innumerable. We now use computers to control them. Tonight, out the window, I can see the trim tabs on the wings rising and falling. With each of their movements the plane rocks slightly, as if in sleep. A few minutes earlier the flaps dropped down 10 degrees, then 20; now, at 40 degrees, they rest, fully extended. The wind rushes loudly around them. The port and starboard wing lights flash, quickly, brilliantly; the wing tip spotlight beyond my window swings out from its nesting place, cutting a swath of light through the dark rain, and slowly rotates upward to illuminate the final approach. Everything is in motion here. Yet the result is an equilibrium of forces, in which aluminum and kerosene and steel ride smoothly downward through the rain.

And below at 500 feet, perhaps a half mile out, we begin to see the dark whitecaps. Like us, they trim themselves to the wind. Tabs of froth peel back from the waves, rising and falling in the surging or ebbing air. They show us what, encased in our calm fuselage, we cannot feel—the turbulence of motion, the raw power of driven water and of the air that even now is pouring from our Rolls-Royce engines. Turbulent, rhythmic, the whitecaps dance beneath us to the shore; breaking over the rocks, they retreat, return, break again, retreat, as we leave them behind for the deep blue lights of runway 28R. For we are home now, beyond the dark water, bowing toward our carry-on luggage as the dance concludes.

I wonder, after such landings, whether we admire our machines so much simply because of what they do, or because they are our best attempts so far to emulate nature itself. Mirror images: the wind-tossed bay, never emptying, never overflowing, with its turbulent equilibrium; the airplane, in a controlled fall, humming smoothly through the storm, shifting slightly, staying in balance. They are not really mirrors, of course. For all their sophistication, our machines are still clunkers compared to sea and sky and molecule. Yet with our machines we harmonize contradictory forces. We lift our heavy selves into the sky, reconciling gravity to thin air. It would appear to be a kind of hubris, the Icarus complex reenacted in modern alloys, except that—as in nature—the balance is all: For our machines to work, they must reconcile forces, not merely use them.

Is this what our inventiveness comes down to, finally—dancing? Surely these serious achievements cannot ultimately lead to something as frivolous as dancing. But there is nothing frivolous about this dance. We hold ourselves, our lives, in this balance of forces. Accepted the invitation of nature, we kick our heels and fly into the air like creatures especially favored, and descend once again to tell the story. We might almost be dreaming. But leaving the airplane, touching its painted aluminum skin, we can taste salty air, and know that this dance is no dream. 🐘

THE CROWN JOODLES, THE MYSTERIES OF EGG-PIT, AND OTHER JOYS OF BEING A MISPRONUNCIATION EXPERT

Doris Kerns Quinn

D ad's hobby was mispronunciations. ❧ He had been fascinated with them since childhood. ❧ He was particularly partial to the mispronunciations of small children, and those that took his fancy were incorporated into his conversation forever. ❧

There was one garbled pronunciation to which he was especially devoted. This one did not come from a child, however, but from an adult of some standing in the community. This is how it came about.

Dad was raised on a small farm and attended a one-room schoolhouse. On one of his many school days—days packed with learning the three R's and gleaning nuggets of wisdom from "McGuffey's Reader"—a member of the school board visited the little schoolhouse. The teacher, perhaps wishing to impress her pupils with the honor this important man was paying them, invited him to read aloud to her class, handing him a geography book. His eye unfortunately fell on an article about Egypt, and he began to read.

The gentleman was somehow under the impression that this exotic name, Egypt, was pronounced "Egg-pit," and thus he read it, with full confidence, not once, but again and again until the lengthy article was finished. The students—even the smallest of whom knew better—were both consternated and amused. In spite of their barely suppressed giggles, the school board member read doggedly on, ignorant as he was of the cause of this unseemly behavior.

Dad, who was only 8 at the time, was astounded that a grown-up could display such appalling ignorance, especially a member of the school board. He never forgot the incident, or the novel mispronunciation, which quite took his fancy. Perhaps he liked visualizing the nation in question as a huge pit filled with gleaming white eggs. At any rate, he carried this bizarre pronunciation into his adulthood, and of course, "Egyptian" became "Egg-*pit*-ian."

81

Occasionally he would forget himself before company and embarrass us by coming out quite naturally with "Egg-pit."

I believe it was this childhood encounter with the fascination of words mispronounced that started him down the road to his obsession. Other favorites with which he studded his conversation were "joodles," for jewels, "jouse," for juice, "shursh," which he made do for both church and shirts, and "windle-sill." All of these gems, and many others, he gleaned from his own children and grandchildren. And even his nickname, "Bobo," came from a mispronunciation. Two of his grandchildren, when learning to speak, feigned inability to come closer to "Grandpa" than "Bobo." He was pleased with the distortion and encouraged its continuance. Inevitably he became "Bobo" to all of us.

When night fell he would sometimes look out the window and mutter "Duck out there!"—a phrase he had borrowed from his small granddaughter and never returned. It was her wondering comment on the dark enveloping the house—although the first time she said it we *did* look out the window for the duck! And films were forever "flims" because of his grandson's verbal typo.

Two of the grandchildren and their mother came to live with us during World War II. I was in my late teens, and the children showed me scant respect, easily recognizing that I was not a figure of authority. They loved to tease me, because when aroused I would chase them through the house with threats like "When I catch you, I'll knock your stupid heads together!"

It came to pass that sometimes at the dinner table they would look at me from under their mischievous little eyebrows and say softly, "Doris is a skunk." This infuriated their mother, though it didn't bother me; name-calling was not something that got to me. It was things like holding the piano pedals while I was trying to practice that caused the blood to rise. I'm sure my sister didn't care whether they called *me* a skunk or not. She was, however, in horror lest they call some *real* person a skunk. So she finally threatened them with most dreadful punishment if they ever again let this word pass their lips. Therefore a new word had to be invented—a *mispronunciation,* of course, of the original. Doris was now a "skink"; but that soon palled, and I became "dorsy-scorsy," and finally, "scorsy-skink."

Bobo was quite captivated by "scorsy-skink." He felt it showed imagination and wit on the part of his talented grandchildren. From that time forward, anything he found disagreeable was "scorsy-skink," which he eventually mercifully shortened to merely "scorsy." He was hopeful for a while that this new and useful word would make it into the dictionary, and he and the children did their best to spread its use. But somehow it never caught on. People apparently just thought, "Those peculiar Kernses!"—not recognizing true creativity.

The grandchildren, now responsible and sober-suited adults, refuse to believe that they ever called their aunt a skunk or that they ever invented so absurd an expression as "scorsy-skink." But Bobo carried on the tradition, calling things "scorsy" well into his 80s.

And he continued all his life to refer to that ever more important country as "Egg-pit."

83

SNOW
David Winder

It was an unexpected meeting considering our backgrounds: Victor a Nigerian; I a white South African. 🐦 Both of us in New York City as foreign students. 🐦

It was the snowfall that had brought us both to Riverside Park that glistening white morning.

The snow had fallen heavily the night before and I had been impatient for it. True, I had seen snow a few times before but always it had already fallen by the time I finally caught up with it some 20 or 30 miles away.

Through November and much of December cold wet winds whipped off the Hudson River. But it didn't snow. Then some time after midnight, walking home from a Christmas party, my ears were stung by what seemed to be sharp needles of ice. Unpleasant, but because it was a new experience, strangely exhilarating. "Is it snow?" I pleaded. "Sleet," returned the passerby.

And so when it finally came I was pleased for I had not seen snow actually fall from the sky.

I remember stretching my hand out from my tenth floor apartment window and feeling those first snow flakes colder, bigger, and mushier than others had had me believe.

In my enthusiasm and naiveté I stuck my head further out expecting to see hundreds of people leaning out of hundreds of other windows doing precisely the same thing. But the maze of windows that run across the Manhattan sky remained uniformly closed. Of course, I reflected, it's just another winter night to them.

Soon the angular grimy roofs turned clean, soft and white, and a sudden silence, as if all the roaring traffic had been submerged under the weight of the snow, seemed to envelop the neighborhood.

It was the following morning that I met Victor. He was at the foot of some stone stairs in Riverside Park. His hands were deep in his pockets. The activity was all in his face—a look of wild delight as if he was making a surprising discovery.

As I approached ankle deep in snow, he snapped out of his private world and looked suddenly sheepish. His embarrassment melted the moment I picked up a snowball and lobbed it exuberantly at a faraway tree. He must have sensed then he was not alone in his enjoyment of the snow.

I can't recall who spoke first. But it was inevitable that we would soon realize we were strangers in a foreign city.

"I'm from Ni-ge-ri-a," he said, the last syllable booming out in a crescendo of pride and pleasure. I remember at the time thinking it was exotic and dignified.

I wish I hadn't hesitated. I must have seemed unfriendly. But I was nervous that the introduction might lead to a battle of political credentials. Coming to the home of the United Nations I had been made all the more aware of African-sponsored resolutions condemning my country's racial policies.

"I'm from South Africa," I said as evenly as possible hoping my handshake might bridge any political gulf he might have felt between our two nations.

"Oh, South Africa," he said with a nervous chuckle and I realized his embarrassment was more acute than mine. And because it was embarrassment and not hostility, it seemed to convey a special kindness and consideration about him as if he were aware I might feel trapped by his introduction. I sensed he was groping for some diplomatic rescue. He immediately bent down, squished a handful of snow and, as if to indicate the beginning of a game, tossed it at me.

"Last night was the first time I saw snow fall," I volunteered.

"Was it? Same here." He beamed. And then as if he had suppressed his excitement too long he spun around, cartwheeled in the air, and flung himself into the snow yelling ecstatically: "It's wonderful. It's wonderful. It's wonderful." And came up with fistfuls of snow.

I was weak with laughter. It was laughter of pure comic joy. I also realized it was laughter of relief that we had survived the introductions.

When he emerged from the snow he pointed

to my camera? "Would you take a picture of me? I want to send it to my mother in Nigeria. She's never seen snow. In fact, she has never seen ice."

"You mean she doesn't know what an ice cube is?" I asked incredulously.

"That's right. In my village we have no refrigerators. So you see I must write to my mother and tell her about snow. Do you think I can make her understand what it is like?"

"Yes," I said politely, although I was not sure that she would. But I knew that she would feel his joy and I did want him to communicate that. 🐚

WASTELAND YEARS
Wakako Yamauchi

Evacuation was the euphemism for the incarceration of Japanese and Japanese-Americans during World War II. 🐚 "Japanese and Japanese-Americans" is a cumbersome phrase, but it's important to use here because it includes two generations of Japanese in America: first, the immigrants who settled here and were denied citizenship; second, their offspring—Americans by birth. 🐚 This is hard for some white Americans to grasp. 🐚 "A Jap is a Jap" is one of the ugly phrases used in those terrible years. 🐚 Another was "But look what you did at Pearl Harbor." 🐚

The median age of the internees was 17. That means most of us took a civics course and we knew that all people are created equal, and justice and freedom are for everyone, regardless of race, color, or creed. That's what the American Revolution and the Civil War were all about. Then as suddenly as the attack on Pearl Harbor came, we learned something else—a devastating lesson on the politics of economics and racism.

In February of 1942, President Roosevelt signed Executive Order 9066, and without due process the Japanese and Japanese-Americans on the West Coast were herded off to 10 internment camps in the "badlands."

First, the leaders of our communities were arrested and put in "detention centers": Bismarck, North Dakota; Missoula, Montana; Santa Fe, New Mexico; there were others. Later the rest of us were sent to assigned camps, taking only what we could carry. Those who got there earlier advised us to bring boots. "Nothing but snakes, scorpions, and dust out here."

We lived one family to a unit, four units to a barracks, with knotty walls separating us from our neighbors. There was little privacy. Furtive love affairs were conducted in the shadows of barracks and in empty office rooms. Family quarrels were stifled and swallowed. The latrines were the worst: rows of toilets back to back, one long trough for washing, a shower room with six shower heads. The modest met each other coming and going in the early hours of the morning.

We waited in line everywhere: at the mess hall with our tin plates, at the post office, the clinic, the showers, at the canteen, in the blazing sun and cold rain. It got so that wherever a crowd gathered, people automatically got in line.

Rumors flourished. Aside from the sordid gossip, there were terrible stories of the war (most of us had relatives in Japan) and of friends who had disappeared. A family friend, a bachelor, was among the early arrests.

No one knew where he was sent, and no one followed up on his disappearance. Later we heard he died. He'd strayed too near a barbed wire fence and when a sentry called, "Halt!" he either didn't hear or chose not to hear and was shot in the back. A friend had a friend whose father saw it happen.

Some say they had a great time in camp. There were softball games in dusty summer evenings, movies in the firebreak (we carried our own collapsible chairs), talent shows—someone always sang, "Don't Fence Me In"—dances, Sadie Hawkins nights, and even here, forsaken as we were, Boy Scouts worked for their merit badges and on holidays marched proudly with Old Glory fluttering high in the yellow air.

There was always someone to love, someone to hate, someone to envy. Lifelong friendships were made, as well as lifelong enemies. And there were the flaming desert sunsets and incredible mornings—cool and crisp, forever promising renewal.

People, especially our children, ask us now: "Why did you go so docilely?" (Like the questions asked of Holocaust victims: "Why did you go like sheep to slaughter?") We did, that's all. There were some who said, "We must be 200 percent loyal. We must cooperate like true Americans."

Others urged, "Let's fight to the last ditch. This is fascism!" A small group of young men protested individually and spent the war years in prison. Some 40 years later two were exonerated. One died before his vindication.

We know now that powerful groups lobbied to push the Japanese and Japanese-Americans out of rich farmlands and booming flower and produce markets on the West Coast. We also know that plans to incarcerate us were in the making before Pearl Harbor. And we know that there was not one saboteur among us.

By the following February, everyone over 17 was required to fill out a questionnaire that was to pave the way to freedom. "Leave Clearance," it was called. Buried among the questions were two:

27. Are you willing to serve in the armed forces of the United States on combat duty, wherever ordered?

28. Will you swear unqualified allegiance to the United States from any and all attack by foreign or domestic forces and forswear any form of allegiance or obedience to the Japanese emperor, or any other foreign government, power, or organization?

These needed only yes-and-no answers, but the 27th asked our young men to join a combat team and fight for freedom while their families remained impounded. The 28th asked our immigrant parents, who had always been denied citizenship, to forswear allegiance to their native Japan, in short, to become people without a country. The impact of these questions was such that young men were identified as yes-yes and no-no boys.

The yes-yes were committed to register or volunteer for the segregated 442nd Regimental Combat Team. Raised with the principles of honor and obligation by their Japanese parents, these boys went on to bring fame and honor to the 442nd, making it the most decorated regiment in the US Army. The casualties were horrendous, but the mission—to prove unqualified loyalty—was accomplished.

The no-no boys refused to register while their families were incarcerated. They were exiled to yet another camp—the first step toward expatriation. The courage it took to make this stand should not be underestimated.

The questionnaire tore families apart. Ours was not an uncommon family experience.

We had come to Poston, Arizona, together, the six of us. We lost everything in Oceanside, California, but the two armloads we carried to camp. The evening we arrived, my father squatted on the dusty barracks for a long time, shoulders hunched, arms folded, his head deep in shadow. I can see him now.

But this wasn't all that was to happen to my father. With the leave clearance, my sister left for Arkansas to marry a soldier. I went to Chicago to pursue the American Dream (to work in a candy factory), and my brother, a no-no boy, went in search of another American Dream—the liberty-or-nothing dream. He was shipped to Tule Lake, in California, the camp for expatriates and dissidents. My father, mother, and six-year-old sister remained in Poston.

After the devastation of Hiroshima, a chronic illness of my father's returned and flared. When everyone was ordered to leave camp, my mother asked him, "Where will we go?" My father never answered.

I returned for the funeral (my sister was already there), but my brother couldn't get a leave permit from Tule. In a few days we left Poston—among the last to go. My mother held my father's ashes on her lap and remarked that they were still warm. 🐚

THREE SHORT MUSINGS
Alex Noble

Decisions before their time 🐛

How few things demand an immediate decision. I may think that I have a decision to make, but I find that often this is not so at all. The ongoing flow of my experience, if I am attentive to it, has a way of clarifying things which at first might seem obscure or confusing. Many times, tomorrow has shown me that yesterday's "decision" was an illusion. Thinking that I had to decide something was just a misguided effort on my part to try and shape an event that was not ready to be shaped.

Does a caterpillar sit around trying to decide whether or not to be a butterfly? 🐛

Right for me 🐛

I notice how again and again I gravitate toward the activities and pursuits that I enjoy most. Much like water from a mountain spring that finds its way over and around all variety of obstacles to the sea, I continually come home to what I love, to doing those things that have for me an innate happiness. The enjoyment that I feel when I am doing something uniquely mine to do is like a message of affirmation. And this sets me to wondering if, in the final analysis, my genuine enjoyment in something is not an infallible guide to its rightness for me. Even if an activity demands a lot of hard work, there can be an abiding sense of delight in the doing of it.

I think about the many times that I have taken on projects out of a sense of false responsibility or false humility, to appear capable, to please or placate others, to prove a point. But there was no joy, and soon boredom, burden, and even resentment began to take their toll. All of which is teaching me that the question "Do I feel happy about this?" is not a frivolous one. 🐛

Taking another approach ༄

I am unhappy about something, and so I complain about it to myself, and to others. My friends, meaning well, give me sympathy. Their sympathy makes me feel more justified in my misery, and becomes an invitation to even greater unhappiness. I tell my unhappy story so many times that it becomes invincible, impenetrable. I take all the bricks of my grievances and build a doorless, windowless room around myself—a room without light or air. I come to believe in my unhappiness so completely that I do not hear even the words of one or two wise friends who refuse to accept my sorrows, and suggest that I stop complaining and start doing my best with whatever good is at hand.

Then, at last, I realize how ridiculous this all is, and how much time, thought, and energy I have been wasting in fruitless negativism. I know better, and resolve to take another approach. My worst failures at trying to make things better must surely be an improvement over my complaints that refuse to see beyond the problem at hand. As Rabinandrath Tagore puts it: "When my eyes are filled with tears, I cannot see the stars." I come to realize that it is a matter of perspective, that misery and complaint only open the way to more misery and more complaint, whereas diligent hope and uncomplaining optimism clear out the channels of thought so that true ideas can flow freely toward whatever adjustments, corrections, and enlightenment are needed. ༄

HOMELESSNESS: ONE MAN'S STORY
Christopher Nyerges

I used to wonder what it would be like to be home-less, needing to survive "on the street." ❧ Then one day I was in that situation—without a home. ❧ I experienced firsthand the home-less "life style." ❧

I now feel the deepest empathy for anyone in such a miserable situation.

Although my period of homelessness was relatively short, I continue to see a part of myself mirrored in each homeless person I see. I've come to conclude that most programs (private and governmental) designed to help the homeless cannot succeed (i.e., eliminate homelessness), because they fail to cognize, let alone directly address, the root causes of the problem.

How did homelessness happen to me?

I became homeless in the aftermath of a divorce. It was difficult at that time for me to stay focused on clear decision-making. Due to the complex situation surrounding the break-up of the marriage—mortgage arrears, unresolved aspects about the ownership of the home, and bad decisions—I found myself homeless within months of moving out.

Even though I owed money to the bank holding the mortgage, I found I was unable to support myself. At times I found that I just couldn't work. I was self-employed—writing, teaching, publishing, lecturing. Those jobs I did work at seemed increasingly futile. Not knowing how I'd pay the bills, I saw myself lose my house. As if from afar I watched myself go through a living nightmare. Of course, I'm simplifying a miserable, deeply chaotic period of time.

My first "home" when I was homeless was the unused cellar of a residential home in my neighborhood. The cellar was empty, convenient, and inconspicuously located. I'd seen the open door to it when I visited a friend who lived nearby. The house was on a two-level lot. The owner lived and kept his car on the upper level. During the weekends he would sometimes garden in the front yard on the lower level. And so I generally stayed away on weekends.

While living in the cellar, I had to be very quiet. I usually came "home" around 11 p.m. when the owner was asleep. To this day I don't believe he knew I resided in his cellar—with my few bags of clothes, my full backpack, and my hammock.

Although at this time I had no full-time job, I did manage to maintain a few part-time jobs. I struggled to do them. To make myself appear "civilized," I took a long time to clean up. I had no bathroom, but there was a hose just outside the cellar door. I bathed with the hose when no one was around, and I vigorously scrubbed myself clean with my boar-bristle brush. My "toilet" was a hole I dug with my small shovel; occasionally I'd use public facilities.

In the evenings, I'd frequently stay late at inexpensive cafés. Then, having no electricity for TV or light, I'd sneak back into my dark "cave" (as I called it) and quietly crawl into my hammock.

I was never really "on the street" like so many of today's homeless. I did have a roof over my head, even if that roof was the floor of an unsuspecting homeowner's living room. But I still experienced the starkness of no stable home. I stared into the vacuum of all that I took for granted: stability, cleanliness, order, warmth, availability of toilet, bath, hot water, telephone, etc.

During this period I was forced to call on my latent talents. On one hand, I could detachedly view it all as a positive "freedom"-promoting experience — which it was. On the other hand, I realized how limiting such a lifestyle was. No one could easily contact me, and thus dollar-earning possibilities and social activities were nearly nonexistent. Projects of any sort were nearly impossible to implement without some sort of solid home base. So although I was "free" of most home and social responsibilities and the need to "perform" for a boss, that "freedom" was wanting. The large number of "freedom-froms" that I experienced radically limited my number of "freedom-tos."

I constantly attempted to improve my situation by finding ingenious new ways to wash my clothes, to go to the bathroom, to carry my gear less conspicuously, to stay clean.

Eventually I was invited to live in the abandoned lower section of a local house. I was given permission by the caretaker and I paid a small rent and utilities. Although abandoned and unsightly, the lower section of the house was definitely several notches better than the cellar I'd been living in; for example, it had electricity.

Later, I rented a warehouse from a man I'd known for many years. He thought he was renting me an office and storage space, and I wrote into our contract that I could live there. Which I did. At the warehouse fear of "discovery" was no longer an issue.

For most of the previous eight years I had been more or less successfully self-employed. When I became homeless, it was more difficult to maintain any sort of meaningful employment. I did maintain a few part-time jobs. For example, I got a job with a Pasadena church, opening and closing up after services. I also worked as a part-time day camp counselor teaching wilderness survival skills. I'd see hundreds of children and dozens of adults each day. I didn't need to be "neat and clean" to do this and these people did not know where I went at night. My closest friends were extremely supportive. The places I lived—the abandoned cellar, the house, the warehouse —were all possible only because of these friends' support. I was by no means "lonely" or "alone" as a homeless person, but I was embarrassed and determined to get myself out of the situation. My co-workers did not know about it. During this time, there was never a moment when I was not filled with a driving desire to rise up out of homelessness. That constant drive —and help from loving friends—is what forced me to explore viable work possibilities and actively to "find home."

When you have nothing, it is very easy just to go along, day by day, and convince yourself that "things aren't really that bad." I knew that this attitude, although seductive, would be deadly. I knew that to allow myself to settle into "homelessness" and allow my "drive" to slow would mean a prolonged period of misery. I needed not to wallow in the experience, but to learn from it and move on. Thus I made the effort to elevate my thinking and stay active.

I frequently encountered the homeless when I worked at the Pasadena church. I was regularly approached and asked for one form of assistance or another—usually money. These people have very real needs, but I've learned that putting money into their palms will not attend to those needs.

I've often wondered: Is the homeless problem today symptomatic of a greater spiritual crisis, a spiritual void, that has occurred as a result of the largely media-created, me-centered world of consumerism? As I continue

95

to encounter the homeless, I keep coming back to two ideas. One is that much of the solution to homelessness lies deep within the volition of each homeless individual. This is how the problem needs to be solved. The best help is to show someone how to help himself. Mindless giving—without an actual self-help program—is of no real help in the long run.

The second idea is that part of the solution to homelessness also rests within the hearts of those more fortunate individuals who are in a position to help.

My period of homelessness was relatively short. My "recovery" took "only" two years. In my process of recovery—my gaining of the ability once more to seek stable self-employment—each step was shaky. I never took anything for granted. The fear of being homeless again was hard to shake. Rising up from the bottom is V E R Y difficult.

This is where more fortunate individuals can help. We must begin to see that there is not a mass called "the homeless." Instead, these are distinct individuals—our brothers—with distinct problems each requiring unique solutions.

In my interactions with the homeless, I continue to abide by the old Chinese axiom "Give a man a fish and he eats for a day. Teach a man to fish and he eats for life." It takes both sides to make this work. ❧

Asking, Loving
Pierre Pradervand

Soon I will be celebrating the anniversary of a rather important date in my life—the time I dared to start thinking for myself. ❧ This, in turn, led to the most profound changes in my life. ❧ And to even more impertinent questions initiating even more fundamental changes in a long chain that has yet to end. . . . ❧

For one who was brought up with the most profound respect for all forms of authority, from the local policeman to the gardener, from my father to God, that was no mean thing. This whole questioning thing started when I was close to seventeen. Bedridden for some unremembered reason, I read a book pleading the Christian case for pacifism.

Now, a good question is like a very efficient drill. Once it has made a nice, clean, deep hole, you tell yourself it can probably make another one . . . and another one, and so on. The French philosopher Blaise Pascal, once wrote, "Woe unto that man who, at least once in his life, has not questioned everything."

Over the years, I went through an accelerating—and sometimes excruciating—process of challenging accepted views which left no altar untouched, no stone unturned. It caused me to leave my childhood church, my country, my values, radically altered my political beliefs, even my profession. For, as I discovered in Africa, what my sociology professors in Europe had taught me as "scientific" research methods, turned out to be a pair of extremely narrow, Cartesian colored glasses offering a supremely shriveled view of what my former professional tribe terms "social reality."

Yet, however rough the ride, I was, slowly and quite unbeknownst even to myself, developing that uniquely precious privilege: the courage to think for myself.

In a world where ideologies are gnawed by the relentless worm of time;

97

where almost everything is changing, very rapidly and on a worldwide level, in a world where, to quote a leading scientist, "The scientific truth of to-day is the error of to-morrow" and in the world where the multiplication and ever accelerating flow of information transforms the very concept of materially or scientifically established "facts" into tenuous, temporary hypotheses; it is useful and most necessary to be able to think for oneself, untrammeled by the "mind-cuffs" of narrow creed or hardened dogma.

No doubt you will often be alone on this initially steep path. Most people prefer the intellectually less arresting position of a hard-boiled egg at the bottom of a picnic basket, content to doze mentally in the shade. And you will but rarely find the sister-soul to share your highest visions—and so it should be. Nor should you attempt to share the unbroken horizons of your inner ocean with those who have dwelt a whole lifetime at the bottom of a well.

During all my years of searching, strangely enough, there was one belief system I did not even think of challenging till much later on in life, and that was the positivistic scientific belief that we can only discover "reality" via experiments that can be duplicated based on information given to us by the senses.

The day a profound and challenging book of metaphysics made me question *that* belief—well, all the precedent eruptions, intellectual earth-quakes and nightlong anguished searchings appeared in comparison like Sunday School outings. Yet that questioning, once weathered, was also the one that brought with it lasting peace.

During all those years of questioning, doubting and wandering, one truth stood out, unwavering, unshaken (albeit at moments very dimmed) by the relentless tornadoes of questions, doubts, human mockery, death, hunger, famine and a thousand other gaunt specters. And that truth was love. Love which I discovered to be the only reality in the universe that is at the same time its own cause, means and end.

For years, in Africa I saw children rummage in my garbage can. The "Why such injustice?" very quickly became, "Is my love deep and fervent enough to dedicate my whole life to building a world where the economy is motivated by service and cooperation rather than profit, greed and competition?"

In a world which appears plagued by ever-increasing uncertainty, by the hollow chameleon of consumerism, where both prophets of despair and sanity speak of the world's possible annihilation, in such a world, the highest form of the courage to think for oneself may well be the courage to love despite all appearances—to love more intelligently, more compassionately and finally—yes, more joyfully. ❧

A Writer's Reflections
Alan Paton

On the day when death will knock at thy door, what wilt thou offer to him? Oh, I will set before my guest the full vessel of my life—I will never let him go with empty hands. All the sweet vintage of all my autumn days and summer nights, all the earnings and gleanings of my busy life will I place before him at the close of my days when death will knock at my door. Rabindranath Tagore wrote these words in his "Gitanjali."

Words such as these moved Yeats to the depths. Yeats could never have written them, just as Tagore could never have written like Yeats. What they had in common was their love of the word.

I have had a love of the word since I was very young. I also have had a love of the Word, the one that was in the beginning. The first love has been almost perfect, the second imperfect. But even at the age of eighty I still ask that the imperfect love could be perfected. Then I shall give my guest the full vessel of my life.

There are some things that I could read for ever. The 23rd Psalm, George Herbert's "Love," Francis Thompson's "Hound of Heaven," A. E. Housman's "Loveliest of trees . . . ," Blake's "Tiger, tiger, burning bright," some of the stanzas of Tagore's "Gitanjali," some of the stanzas of Fitzgerald's "Rubaiyat," Shakespeare's "The quality of mercy . . . ," Yeats's "The Lake Isle of Innisfree." I often read Vachel Lindsay's "General William Booth Enters Into Heaven" in public, but I don't trust it, because my voice tends to break down when I come to the last seven lines. I apologize for all the things I have left out. I must mention two things more—the "Holy Mountain" of Isaiah, and the "New Heaven and New Earth" of John on Patmos.

Why could I read these poems for ever? I suppose it is because they evoke some deep response from the soul. Perhaps I should exclude the "Rubaiyat" on that account, but it has a beauty all its own, which atones for its philosophy of "let us eat and drink, for tomorrow we die." There are many miracles in man's evolution, but one of the greatest is the word, the beginning of language, and the beginning of literature.

When I look back on my past life, I often marvel at the fact that for my first forty-five years I was a model public servant, honest, industrious, and with a great respect for the authority of the state. For the next thirty-five years I decided that I could not accept the new laws that poured out of the parliament, the laws of apartheid, the laws that were to separate the races of South Africa, and in particular the white race from all others, in every conceivable place and on every conceivable occasion, in trains, buses, hospitals, hotels, schools, universities—the list is endless. Mixed racial marriages are unlawful. In 1953 we founded the Liberal Party of South Africa, which decided to oppose these laws by every possible means, except those of violence; and also to oppose the harsh new security laws, which were ostensibly intended to control communism, but in fact were intended to control and destroy any kind of opposition to apartheid.

I was very nervous about my decision to use my writing and my speaking to oppose the government. I did not take up the task of opposition with a glad cry. I was committing an act of defiance, and I didn't like it. But the alternative was to become a pseudo-Christian. Therefore I decided to defy.

From that day my life changed. Wherever I went, to Durban, or Cape Town, or Johannesburg, the security police were waiting for me. We did not speak, but each knew who the other was. They would park their cars outside my house. On one occasion they searched me and the house. They knew my every movement. They warned me that I was running the risk of being "banned" under the Suppression of Communism Act. This was a supreme irony, because I abhorred the doctrines of Marx-Leninism. When a niece of mine died in Pietermaritzburg, they attended the funeral. They did not join the mourners, but stood outside their cars, with hard implacable faces. Their presence did not please my niece's family who were formal and conservative. I felt I should not have gone.

My life was like that for fifteen years. But others paid much more for their beliefs, because, I presume, they were not so well-known. Mr. Peter Brown, once chairman of the Liberal Party, was banned from public life for ten years. To a large extent he was banned from private life also. He could not be present at the birthday parties of his own children, because he was forbidden to "attend any gathering." Helen Joseph, Winnie Mandela, Mewa Ramgobin, and many others paid this heavy price. Banning affects different people in different ways, but not one of them abandoned his or her beliefs.

In 1968 the government made it a criminal offence for any member of one racial group to make common political cause with any member of another group. In no circumstances could the Liberal Party have broken up into separate racial parties. Therefore we disbanded. We had our farewell meeting at the Caxton Hall, Durban. I told the security police, of whom there were eight present, that for fifteen years I had pretended to be indifferent to their continuous surveillance, but that in fact I had not liked it at all. Since that night in 1968 I have not seen them again. Others have not been so lucky.

Well that's enough of sorrow. My life has been happy rather than sorrowful. I could recount my blessings but there's not enough space.

Has life taught me any lessons? Many, but especially one. And that is that the only way to make man's inhumanity to man endurable, is to try to exemplify in our lives man's humanity to man. Jesus taught that long ago, and so did Francis, so did Ignatius, and many others.

What is the future of my country? It will become a non-racial country, but whether by painful evolution or by cataclysm, no one knows. If by cataclysm, the blacks will recover, the whites never. 🐚

Tangling With Technology
Barbara Tuchman

In the course of recent political oratory, one speaker (I don't remember who it was) assured us that his party's program would prevail because (I quote), "Americans are a smart people." ✍ I wonder about that. ✍ Is it in fact true? ✍

It had struck me during the campaign that the American people, rather than showing themselves smart, were in fact remarkably gullible and ready to accept almost any proposition that was offered from beneath a handsome head of hair. If the speaker was personable, friendly, and skilled in delivery, he could, through access to the mass media, build up a following and carry his followers to acceptance of, and vehement belief in, any empty set of platitudes. Viz. Gary Hart's platform of hearty if unspecified "new ideas," which seemed to me the gauziest wings of political oratory heard in modern times and yet carried his public to warmest enthusiasm; see also Mr. Reagan's dizzy exercise in 180-degree turns which led him to say first one thing and then its opposite so smoothly that the public, following faithfully along, noticed no discrepancy.

The agent of these performances is a technological instrument developed to such wondrous perfection as to be actively harmful, because it can make a candidate for public office appear twice, no, 10 times as intelligent as he really is and seemingly worthy to be entrusted with the complex and difficult decisions of national policy. As such, the teleprompter becomes as dangerous as a nuclear warhead. Through its means, an oaf becomes knowledgeable, a bore becomes interesting, an ignoramus becomes an expert, and the public swallows it all without for a moment asking itself how this person, so skillfully delivering the prefabricated sentences unrolling on the tape before him and invisible to us, would perform in the hard sessions of the Oval Office.

The public does not ask itself this question—it does not think about it, it forms a judgment and then votes on the basis of a mechanical trick and on the assumption that this nice fellow, so attractively packaged as if he were a product of the advertisers' art (which indeed he is), will do fine once he is given charge. To believe that is not smart. Rather it is on a par with the visitor to the coronation who saw the hawk-nosed Duke of Wellington, in coronet and robes of velvet and ermine, emerge from the Abbey and ask him politely, "I beg pardon, Sir, are you Mr. Smith?" "If you believe that," replied the Duke, "you will believe anything."

I thought about the smartness question when I was visited by a group of behavioral scientists who wished to show me the results of an elaborate study they had made of the diplomatic telegrams that passed among the foreign offices of Paris, Vienna, Berlin, London, and Moscow, in July 1914. Each of the messages had been numerically rated down to decimal points, as I remember, according to degrees of expressed hostility and then fed into the computer. When assembled after months of meticulous work the output filled three mimeographed volumes which reached the conclusion that the likelihood of war rose in direct proportion to the rising degree of hostility. This astonishing discovery had not been hidden from a generation of ordinary historians who had studied the material without electronic assistance. We are being bemused by computers and their supposed omnipotence. In fact, they are like sociologists who after painstaking reduplicated research always produce a conclusion—for instance, that women are less likely to be mass-murderers than men, or that school truancy shows a correlation with fatherless homes—that everyone knows already from everyday observation.

I am not a sociologist, not even a behavioral scientist, that new breed, but only what has been designated an "intuitive historian" (a phrase I rather welcome); yet from this modest stand I would venture the proposition that computers, while enormously useful and informative, may be making us in a fundamental sense less smart, that is to say less able to exercise intuitive knowledge, than we have formerly been.

Here is where I see a danger—in that the greater the technologies we develop for purposes of general homicide or genetic control or space travel, the less wisdom we will have for managing them.

History has foreshadowed this problem before now. Discussing the origins of World War I, George Kennan in his book "The Fateful Alliance," published this year, writes that "one sees [in those years] the growth of military technological capabilities to levels that exceed man's capacity for making any logical and intelligent use of them." I jumped when I read that, because 10 years ago when writing my book "A Distant Mirror," I had concluded the same thing from an incident in the 14th century.

In 1386, in the course of the Hundred Years' War, the French planned a massive invasion of England intended to achieve a second Norman Conquest. It was to be transported by an armada planned to be the greatest "since God created the world." The armada was assembled in the wide bays at the mouth of the Scheldt on the Flemish coast. Ships of every kind from barges to galleons hired or purchased from all over the Continent from Prussia to Castile crowded the sea lanes converging on the meeting place, while on land an endless train of arms, men, equipment, and provisions filled the boats. Barrels of biscuits and wine, of salt fish and dried beans, hundreds of live beef cattle, sheep, and fowl, casks of olive oil, cases of cheeses, sugar and nuts, everything from hand-mills for grinding wheat to gangplanks for horses, from stone cannon balls to catapults and flamethrowers, from gunpowder to 200,000 arrows, from urinals to timber for making carts was thought of.

The most stupendous of all the preparations was a portable town to protect and house the invaders upon landing. A huge camp enclosing a place for each captain and his company, it was virtually an artificial Calais to be towed across the Channel. Its dimensions epitomized the fantasy of omnipotence. It was to have a circumference of nine miles and an area of 1,000 acres surrounded by a wooden wall 20 feet high, reinforced by towers at intervals of 12 and 22 yards. Houses, barracks, stables, and markets where the companies would come for their provisions were to be laid out along prearranged streets and squares. Nothing so daring in concept and size as this had ever been attempted. Prefabricated in Normandy by the work of 5,000 woodcutters and carpenters, supervised by a team of architects, it was to be packed and shipped in numbered sections, so designed that assembly at the beachhead could allegedly be accomplished in an unbelievable three hours.

In the end this triumph of technology never served its purpose, for, owing to political divisions in the French camp between the peace party and the war party, the great armada never sailed. Preparation in spirit and will did not match the marvel of material. Decision for departure was postponed so often that the winter months came, foreclosing the expedition, while disaster smote the portable town. Loaded aboard 72 ships, it was on its way from

105

Rouen to the Scheldt when the convoy was attacked by an English squadron and three of the French ships were captured along with the master carpenter in charge of construction. Two of the ships were towed to England and their sections of the amazing edifice intended for the beachhead were exhibited in London, to the awe and triumph of the English. In writing of the fate of this stillborn colossus, I was moved to comment, "For belligerent purposes, the 14th century, like the 20th, commanded a technology more sophisticated than the mental and moral capacity that guided its use."

With respect to a nuclear arms race, that conclusion is now one we cannot escape.

At any high-powered conference today of planners and thinkers on nuclear strategy, one can hear the sharpest brains impressively discussing the capabilities of first strike, launch on warning, target fratricide, and every variety of lethal deployment, all in the name of deterrence. The intellectual powers expended are high, while the object, which presumably is to prevent war by increasing the amount of weapons and perfecting their use, is unintelligent, not to say futile. It only stimulates the opponent himself to increase and perfect his arms in a race for superiority—which, if gained, whoever the winner, would last about a week.

How can we turn aside this devotion of our best intelligence to sterile and fruitless ends? If the French of the 14th century put their best efforts into the largest conceivable instrument of war they could muster, its loss was a portent, for in the end France was invaded and occupied by the enemy. I am not suggesting that our concentration on material will end the same way, but I *am* suggesting that it is not the way to achieve the desired end, namely the avoidance of war.

Why cannot the sharpest brains and most creative intellects be applied not to weaponry that can only be destructive, but to determining the cause of the quarrel and defusing it? What in fact *is* the cause for war with the Soviet Union? It is, as I see it, simply fear of each other, and when each of two parties fears attack the impulse is to knock the other fellow out before he can strike you.

It seems to me as obvious as daylight that we would be more usefully engaged in dismantling this fear than in devising ever more injurious means of arousing it. The Russians, with a long and painful experience of hostile invasion from the Mongols to Napoleon to the Germans in World War II, have a natural and understandable fear of enemy attack by the noncommunist

106

world, whose focus they see in the United States, and not without reason, given the intemperate language and off-the-cuff weekend jokes of our chief of state. They think our technical science will someday produce the omnipotent weapon that will pierce their defenses. We fear that Communist subversion will gradually control neighboring and contiguous countries around our shores until we are encircled by a ring of revolutionary threat that can only be countered by making an end of the Soviet system at the center.

This phobia about red revolution is old and innate in a society of haves, and with far less reason than the Russians' fear of invasion. It does not take a historian to recognize that social revolution as shown in the three major cases of the modern era, the French, the Russian, and the Chinese, grew out of the intolerable misery and oppression of the great mass of working people and that, as regards this condition, the U.S. is as far from revolution in the Marxist sense as chocolate cake from green cheese. Not 47 or 147, or however many Communists Joe McCarthy claimed were hiding in the State Department, could make it happen if the social condition is not present. Why people on the right are so afraid of it and shake in their shoes at the least sign of socialist agitation in Central America seems to me evidence that we are not really as smart as some of us like to think.

Rather than continuing to tramp forward with blind confidence in technological hardware, should we not instead be summoning the most intelligent political minds equipped with a sense of realities to force into the open, if possible, some honest examination in human terms with the Russians of our mutual fears which might render them inoperative? We might even allay the tension upon discovering that there was in fact no imminent cause for conflict and that neither do we intend to foment a general attack upon them nor do they seriously intend, in other than theory, to conquer the world. If the best efforts of the best minds were applied to this end, surely it would be a safer and less expensive way to prevent war than risky experiments in games of deterrence.

The experts say you cannot talk to the Russians in human terms because they are too mistrustful and too tied in knots of Politburo directives. Yet Americans must find a way to reach them, for endless haggling over details of so-called disarmament may succeed in discarding or restricting some weapons but not the intentions behind the weapons, which is all that matters. If we cannot subdue the quarrel, we are getting nowhere, while relying on grandeur and excess of materiel could lead us to the same sad futility of the 14th century portable town. 🐚

SWILL
John Gould

Swill is a word the generations have eliminated from our customs and our language, and this is a shame. ⮞ That swill and garbage may be used one for the other in a certain meaning is granted, but back in the days of a rurally oriented people, we knew only swill. ⮞ Now the differences are several. ⮞

For one thing, swill seems to have taken on a negative sound, and the truly genteel perfected a preference for garbage. Gurth and Wamba talked about this back along, noticing that words for animals are usually Anglo-Saxon, whereas the better set likes to use Norman words for the products. Pigs, swine, hogs in the barnyard, but pork on the table. Beef from cows; mutton from sheep.

So swill seems to derive from Old English, but garbage is Roman. In my youth we knew nothing about garbage, but swill was useful and we never wasted it. The kitchen sink had a swill dish—a basin with drain holes. Table scraps went into it, and regular trips were made to the barn and henhouse to empty it. Everybody had biddies and everybody kept a pig.

In swill days there were no garbage problems, and because we had hens and hogs we lacked many another problem, too. Look up the word *ort*. Ort left the language before swill did; anybody cleaning up after supper put the orts in the hens' swill dish, and they were recycled, except that we didn't know about recycling.

The euphuism that fetched on garbage made its own new distinction —garbage is useless. Swill was as good as money in the bank. In my youth I carried swill to the hens, and now that we have no animals, I take it to my compost heap and get the good of it. Waste not, want not. Today hereabouts a man comes once a week to carry my neighbors' garbage to the sanitary landfill.

When my father arose the morning of his 75th birthday anniversary he did not know that a little party had been arranged by his friends and neighbors, and that they would gather in the evening to help him get accustomed to that new number.

Such things need to be a secret, so after supper there had to be some kind of subterfuge to get Father out of the house while the assembly formed and the cake was lighted on the sideboard. My mother, not otherwise given to deceit, used the swill dish as the excuse. Instead of putting the orts from supper therein, she kept them aside and out of sight, dumping them in at just the right time and saying, "Oh, Frank—you forgot to take out the swill!"

Frank mumbled that he'd looked and "they warn't none," but the house rule forbade orts in the sink overnight. Dusk was due and the world on the edge of night. Dad grabbed the swill dish while there was yet time, scooted through the kitchen door into the shed, and gained the henhouse just as the birds had decided to settle on the roosts for the night. They wondered what had happened to their postprandial provender, and decided it was a lost cause.

They were delighted when Dad appeared to toss their swill on the henhouse floor, and they scrambled down to partake. The joyful manner in which hens approach nourishment is a profound experience in unbounded gratitude.

Dad, in the midst of his flock, appreciated the remarks and stood there in the dim light for a moment until each hen had spoken in full. He was about to return to the house (and the party, except that he didn't know there was to be a party) and all at once he realized that he hadn't picked up the day's donation of eggs.

He stepped carefully through the pecking hens to gain the row of nests on the far wall, and felt into each nest and filled the swill dish with what he found. The swill dish was just full, so he held it in the palm of one hand and protected the eggs with the other. Gingerly and gently he made his way out, hasping the door, coming across the barnyard, and entering the dark shed to come to the kitchen door.

Everybody was there, and an attentive ear heard him coming. A voice whispered, "All ready! Here he comes!" At this, the kitchen door was flung open wide and everybody began to sing "Happy birthday to you, happy birthday to you," etc. The swinging door took care of the 17 fresh eggs in the swill dish. They began seeping through the drain holes onto my father's over-alls and onto the shed floor.

My father's surprise-party remarks were not heard above the singing, which was good, and then he sportingly removed his overalls and hove them after the swill dish into a corner. He washed up at the sink and then blew out the candles. I merely submit that the word "garbage" never brought on a memory of suchlike. 🐖

THE FORMS
OF LOVE

THE BIRD OF PARADISE CORSAGE
Paul Hunter

The birds-of-paradise are now blooming in profusion in Los Angeles. 🐦 You see them everywhere: in front of homes, in front of office buildings, in the center dividers along Wilshire Boulevard. 🐦

For some reason, they keep reminding me, this year, of a corsage I gave a girl in college.

An exotic flower, the bird-of-paradise looks like the head of a bird. Its bright orange and blue flowers protrude like feathers from a pearlish gray sheath which ends in a point like a beak. It makes a dramatic corsage. You might even say bizarre.

My father once gave such a corsage to my mother. I saw it in the refrigerator the next morning and stared at it in awe. My mother told me it was beautiful, and naturally I went through life believing her.

The recipient of my corsage was a tall, blond girl with a bright intelligence and quick sense of humor. We were tentatively interested in each other, and I expected to fall in love at this big dance. The corsage was a kind of symbolic declaration of intentions.

She opened the box with anticipation. I can see her now in a beautiful blue organdy dress, standing in the entry hall of her dormitory. When she saw the corsage, she said, "What is it?" and started to laugh.

I knew I was not going to fall in love that night.

Now I realize she reacted in a predictable way. She was from Chicago; we were in a small college town in southern Illinois. She'd never seen a bird-of-paradise before. To her it wasn't a beautiful, tropical flower. It was science fiction.

I detested the whole corsage ritual. I hated having to decide what kind of flower to give a girl. It was so hard to be imaginative. And if you really cared, didn't you owe it to the girl to be imaginative? To separate her from the crowd as you did in your mind?

One of my friends always gave the girl of the moment "one perfect, long-stemmed rose." It had something to do with the rose's perfection matching her own. I thought it was cheap. He thought it was romantic.

The girls always thought so, too—at least at first. But by the end of the dance, the rose would be dangling wearily in the girl's hand like a leash without a dog, and I'd wonder: Hasn't she gotten tired of holding that thing? Wouldn't she like to put it somewhere—in her hair, in her teeth, in the garbage?

One different drummer type considered the whole business worthy of satire. Before one dance, he gathered some dandelions, tied them with a broken shoelace, and presented them to his date.

She was equal to it. She put on the corsage and spent the evening going up to people, and saying, "Don't you love my corsage! Dave made it himself!"

The dance at which I expected to fall in love was held in the outdoor pavilion of a summer resort on the Mississippi River just over the hill from college. It was a balmy spring evening; a band was playing soft, sweet music; the moon was shining on the river. But I was feeling cheated.

The reason was the girl who kept making jokes about her bird-of-paradise corsage. Someone would ask her about it, and she'd say, "You better like it 'cause if you don't, I'll take it off and stab you with it!" I was the only one who wasn't laughing.

We went out together a few more times. She was lovely, really, but the magic was gone.

What do you suppose would have happened if I'd given her a gardenia? 🐚

STRANGERS ON A TRAIN
Kevin H. Siepel

When I first saw her in the station at St. Margrethen she was boarding the railroad car in which I sat, shoving an enormous brown leather suitcase up the high step with her knee. 🐚

Earth colors she was wearing: pants of brown corduroy, knitted vest patterned in orange and brown, Kelly green shirt with uprolled sleeves. Dark eyes, dark hair, dark complexion, young, mysterious. After heaving her burden onto the overhead rack, she collapsed into a seat across the aisle from me, perspiring sedately. Then the silver, air-conditioned train quietly sealed itself to continue its five-hour run westward across Switzerland.

Alpine streams boiled with icy meltwater, and the fields were ablaze with poppies, for the month was May. I attempted first to doze, then to strike up a conversation with the person next to me. No success there. I tried to doze a second time and couldn't, and then I noticed her again. She had produced a posy of wilted wildflowers from somewhere, and was now holding it on her lap, her thoughts apparently upon whoever had given it to her. She had a strong but tranquil face. She was looking at the flowers and lightly smiling. I moved across the aisle and sat down facing her.

"Wie heissen die Blumen?" I asked. I knew that the salad bowl of German words at my disposal would not get me far. Perhaps speaking to her at all was a mistake. At any rate her only answer to my question about the flowers was a smile. Ah, I thought, not German. Italian, of course. She's dark.

I leaned forward to craft a more careful question about *i fiori,* knowing that if the conversational terrain should dip in that direction I'd have to beat an even quicker retreat. She still didn't answer me. The thought that she was mute crossed my mind, but I dismissed it. Since this was Switzerland, I had a final choice: French. The reply, however, was as before: a Mona Lisa smile. I began to wonder. I'd seen a stationful of Yugoslavs in Buchs that morning, back toward the Austrian border. Could she be one of them? The prospect of hearing her speak at last in Serbo-Croatian was discouraging. Better to go slowly now.

I leaned back, relaxed, and returned the smile as enigmatically as I could. I tried to look mysterious—a foredoomed task, considering my garb of crushable fisherman's hat, red long-john shirt, pinstriped mustard slacks, and leather running shoes. It didn't work. Just as I was about to pack it in, Mona Lisa spoke. *"Habla español?"* she asked. Why hadn't I thought of it? She's Spanish! A tourist, maybe, but more likely a *Gastarbeiter*. There were loads of Spaniards working in Switzerland.

With all circuits snapping to life, I strove to call up my meager store of Spanish while rummaging frantically through my bag for the right Grosset's phrase book. I commenced to address this person whose national origins were beginning to take form. She turned out indeed to be a Spaniard, on her way home to see her family. She was single, employed in a home for the aged in Alstätten, and incredibly, her suitcase was stuffed with Swiss chocolate.

Our conversation, unfortunately, was hampered by more than language difficulties, since I had been ill for 24 hours and was still required to take periodic and sudden absences. She proved to be understanding. She turned out, however, to be a poor judge of national costume or accents, taking me first for an Englishman and later for a German. I was apparently the first specimen she'd encountered from the Land of the Free and the Home of the Brave.

What we spoke of, exactly, I can't remember, but the day flew past, and I do recall we were in marvelous accord on a number of important issues. I dreaded our arrival in Geneva, where we would part, but by day's end we were there. We strolled for a while through the city's pretty streets, dallied over *cappuccino* in a sidewalk café, inspected shop windows in the day's failing light, laughed together, and filled conversational voids with banalities until my train came. Hers was due later, at midnight. I said goodbye with great reluctance. She appeared to share my feeling, but her people were beckoning from across the Pyrénées, and my schedule called me to Italy before returning home. We exchanged addresses. I then boarded the train and left.

Today my life doesn't have the broad margin it had then. Like many other people I raise children, commute, remodel, and mow the lawn. But I sometimes think of those days, when life could become so quickly and intensely bittersweet, when great possibilities could yawn in an instant.

115

In fact, one way I'm able to retain perspective on the here and now is by recalling the details of that particular spring day, with its chance meeting and sad goodbye. Occasionally I've recounted the event to others, too, but there I enjoy taking some liberties with the facts, making the girl somewhat more desperate and myself a bit more dashing or distant. In one of my versions the girl unabashedly pursues me. My wife especially enjoys hearing me carry on in this vein.

Even though she likes the story, my wife does find its variations astonishing. She insists that on the train she was not desperate, that I was not distant or dashing, and that she left Switzerland the following year to marry me despite the way I was dressed that day. ❧

The Terrace
Fredeic Hunter

For a day or two, I am alone in the apartment we will soon be leaving. 🐘 Donanne has gone to visit her parents in Santa Barbara. 🐘 She wants to tell her mother about the new apartment so that they can arrange our furniture together in their minds. 🐘 They will coo over the added space a second bedroom will give us and probably decide that we should be loaned some of my parents-in-law's furniture, pieces they do not really need. 🐘 I suspect that this was the real purpose of the trip. 🐘

Although I lived in this apartment for two years as a bachelor, I am no longer used to being here alone. The strangeness of it, combined with the imminence of our departure, causes moments of reminiscence to capture me. None concerns the bachelor period, and I suppose that fact indicates my satisfaction with the fourteen months of married life we have spent here.

Though many occasions drift through my mind, it is— unexpectedly— the terrace I think about most frequently. It is hardly more than a large balcony. Still, it is private and almost airborne in feeling, and it offers a view, not only of other apartment roofs but of sky and eucalyptus trees and city lights— if you stretch your neck enough at night. It is the highest terrace on the pool side of this multi-level building. I recognized it as one of the features of the apartment from the time I rented it. Even so, it remained unused and bare throughout the entirety of my single existence here. It took a wife to transform it.

As I remember, Donanne first cast an appraising woman's eye upon it the day, shortly before we were married, when we repainted the bedroom. We were munching on sandwiches, our faces spotted white from the backfly of paint from the rollers, the lunch tray balanced on an upended apple crate. We were sitting on folding chairs, beloved relics handed down from my parents, when Donanne took note of the splendid emptiness about us. "Don't you ever use this terrace?" she asked.

I had no outside furniture, I explained, though sometimes I did drag a chair onto the terrace in order to read. But not very often.

"Don't you ever eat out here when it's nice?"

As far as I could remember, this was the first time.

"Hmm. We could do something with this space, you know," she said. "It would be lovely here in the summer."

Three weeks later we were married. Not long after, there appeared on the terrace ledge certain bits of pottery: a terra-cotta tile with a sombreroed man painted on it, a tiny blue vase (which has not held a single flower there), a flat rectangular dish and a flat elliptical one which have acted as birdbaths after rains and when we remembered to fill them, and, strangest of all, a pottery salt cellar in the form and hue of a mushroom.

It was the mushroom which led me to observe that the pottery struck me as rather quaint. I learned that it was family pottery. "It's no quainter than your folding chairs," my wife said.

She was right, I saw, and the bits of pottery stayed just as the folding chairs had.

A small barbecue we had received as a wedding present soon joined them. Then a sack of charcoal briquets and a can of charcoal lighter. We began to have dinner on the terrace, alone and with friends, a card table replacing the upturned apple crate. We dined with all the amenities: with a tablecloth and candles, a glowing barbecue and quaint pottery on the ledge. It was very pleasant. We could look off across the evening toward the murmuring eucalyptuses.

Soon sound came regularly from the terrace: tinkling. Donanne had installed a glass wind bell (a family wind bell) on a hook which protruded from the overhanging roof. But I was still thinking a bit like a bachelor, and now and then the bell disturbed my concentration. Did it have to be so incessantly joyful? But I said nothing. It was happy and so were we. Maybe I should concentrate on that.

Then suddenly the terrace was fully furnished. Some of my wife's relatives moved, and we found ourselves with a chaise and a rocker for the terrace, with geraniums and flowering succulents. One of these, five feet tall,

118

leaned from its corner like a hungry carnivore toward anyone who sat on the terrace.

We began to spend a good deal of time out there. Birds visited us, for the birdbath and the redwood seeds we were trying to grow. (Redwoods, we found, did better in the kitchen.) Insects visited, too. One noon Donanne noticed a bee entering the small length of tubing used to support one of the succulents, apparently building a nest. For several weeks, he flew a regular route to and fro, and on the inbound trip he usually carried a geranium petal. You would see a spot of pink hovering above, then descending into the tube to emerge seconds later as a bee. We did not know that bees built nests (we are still unclear on this point), but it would certainly be fun, we agreed, to nap on geranium petals.

Soon now we must leave the terrace, gather up the quaint pottery and the plants, haul out the furniture. Wind has long since silenced the tinkling bell. Shards of it now rest in the pottery vase that never held a flower for us, and, since discarding them seems hard, we have vague intentions of repairing the bell for some further use at the new apartment.

We are not sorry to move. Quite independently of each other we decided that now was the time to do it. We found the new place almost before we started looking and leased it the next day. Its terrace does not match the present one, but it has new carpets and new draperies and closet space galore. We are very pleased with it.

I know we will not soon forget the terrace we are leaving. We had one of our last lunches on it a day or two ago, and I could not help remembering then the first lunch we ate there. We had been dating for a year and a half and thought we knew each other well, at least well enough to get married on.

Thinking back to that first lunch out there, I realized that we had hardly known each other at all. What we knew and loved then was like that empty terrace. It contained mostly potential. We did not know that then, of course. But we do now. Our lives have filled as the terrace has: not simply with things, but with visitors and memories, with friends and living things. That is one of the reasons we will not soon forget the terrace. 🐚

Joy From An Infant Planet
Owen Thomas

We knew all about how new parents talk too much about their children—we'd seen the sitcoms, the New Yorker cartoons. 🐚 I'd even joked with friends that I might not be able to keep myself from telling them about burps and diapers and his (or her—we didn't know) tiny little *perfect* little hands and feet. 🐚 You'll have to warn me, I said, when I get boring. 🐚

Six weeks later, we came to our senses.

We realized that everyone was just waiting to hear about the cute noises he makes, how he hunches over when you burp him, how he looks like a little frog in his crib. How he can smile now, and how he stretches and scrunches after a nap. And his nicknames —did I mention nicknames? "Milk Turtle," "Pound Puppy," "Cuddle Bucket," "Sly Squirrel." There are more. So why do you suppose our carpenter—someone we considered our friend—nodded and backed away with a semifrozen smile when we explained to him how the doctor, too, saw right away what an exceptional child he was, how we think he has grayblue eyes for keeps, now, how soft the soles of his feet are, and . . .

In saner moments I realize I've gone right over the edge with this child: I stare at him so hard I can hardly tell what he looks like—I can only concentrate on one part of his face at a time. And he beams back up at me, hardly blinking, drinking in. I see expectant couples now and say, in my green wisdom, "Oh, they may *think* they know what they're in for. . ."

I thought I knew. I thought I knew. But a door opened, a door closed, and I must be on a different planet.

His eyes were open, I think—I know he looked at me—and he was crying so hard his chin was shaking. (We made a point of asking the doctor, later: "Did you slap our precious child? Is *that* why he was crying?" He said no, no, no, he hadn't done anything, it's probably the change in air pressure or the change in temperature, or just the child saying—and here he looked up, spread his arms wide, and waved his head back and forth—"Is *this* what I was promised!" He was a little wild from having been up all night delivering babies, I think.)

So our child is crying, and I'm crying, and my wife is crying, and the doctor says jollily, "Well, that's a good sign—a good, healthy cry gets the lungs filled up." Sometime later, while we're still marveling at this amazing thing and are hardly noticing, the doctor says a little less jovially, "Well, that's about enough crying for now . . ." He kept on a while after that. We didn't mind.

Seven weeks later, I have begun apologizing to friends. I'm training myself, in conversations, to start with the most amazing recent events—his smiles, perhaps, or his turning over by himself. I blurt them out, then check for a response: If their eyes don't light up, just a little, I pry myself onto another topic. But if there's the slightest raised eyebrow, the encouraging "He *did*?" I let them have it. They must be from my new planet, too. ✺

Animal Crackers In My Purse
Diane Manuel

Minutes before the interview was due to begin, I glanced down at my hands—and almost turned the color of the stains on both thumbs. ❧ Fingerpaint purple, no doubt about it. ❧

"Shiny purple!" I could still hear my three-year-old son shouting from the kitchen earlier that morning. He'd just discovered what happens when you mix red and blue fingerpaint with your elbows, and he wanted the immediate neighborhood to share in his excitement. Now the Korean artist I was about to interview would see the results of our cleanup project.

It wasn't the first time I'd shown up at a business appointment sporting some reminder of the haphazard dual existence I lead—as full-time mom and part-time free-lance writer. I'd had other, more embarrassing moments, like the time I'd taken off my raincoat in a fashionable executive suite and discovered I was wearing several of my son's Mickey Mouse stickers. Still, each new faux pas adds to the list of occupational hazards of being self-employed.

When our son was born and I decided to stop working full time and become a free-lancer, it seemed like a fairly uncomplicated decision. My husband and I thought we could easily turn the laundry room at home into an office where I'd be able to work for hours on end while the baby slept or played contentedly at my feet.

Three years later, my desk still backs up to a washer and dryer in a basement room off the garage. Several dictionaries and a thesaurus compete for space with fabric softeners on an improvised bookshelf. The baby has grown into an independently minded preschooler who demands equal time on the typewriter—and whose paragraphs often make as much sense as mine.

With no regular office hours, I try to make the most of whatever spare time I have. This means doing my writing after Jonathan goes to bed at night, making phone calls during his afternoon nap, and snatching up every 10-minute distraction I can when he's awake. Let him get launched into a building project with his blocks, and I deftly tear a page from one of his coloring books and start jotting down thoughts for an overdue book review.

When deadlines creep perilously close and I need an extra half-hour or two, I occasionally let him plunder the kitchen cabinets while I try to make sense of my scattered pages. I've even been known to turn him loose in the children's section of our local library while I do a last-minute checking of facts. Actually, we have three nearby libraries to choose from, and so can spread our visits around. Jonathan either gets to climb on top of the dollhouse at the Marshfield library, scatter jigsaw-puzzle pieces at the Hanover library, or bang away on the child-size typewriter at the Norwell branch. The children's librarians love to see us coming.

Although I prefer to do as much work as I can at home, there are times when interviews are unavoidable. Those days I brush the modeling clay off my Sunday shoes, remove the Sesame Street cassette from my tape recorder, and head out into the world beyond the playroom. Unfortunately, I have trouble remembering to tidy up my purse.

As a relatively inexperienced mom, I tend to carry more than the usual complement of toys and distractions. There are always a coloring book or two in my purse, a box of crayons, and equally essential bags of raisins and animal crackers. I also pack along a number of small cars, depending on Jonathan's favorite vocation of the month. When he's into his fireman mode, it's fairly simple to bring a tiny hook and ladder truck. When he tells me he's pretending to be an electric company, it's a bit more challenging to come up with the necessary equipment.

I'm not complaining. It's just that when I slip my hand into my purse in the middle of an interview, searching for a pen, I never know what I'm going to come up with. Sometimes it's Jonathan's bright yellow robot, the one that turns into a monstrous praying mantis with a few flicks of the wrist. Too often, I discover a long-forgotten apple.

When I'm not rummaging through my purse, I often spend a good portion of my interviews trying to dicipher the questions I've jotted down ahead of time. Because I use the same notebooks for last-minute grocery lists, I constantly have to guard against posing questions from the wrong page. It's one thing asking a well-known actress about the influence of her childhood pretending on some of her latter-day roles. It's quite another inquiring if she prefers chunky or creamy peanut butter.

Sometimes, however, the most unexpected conversations have resulted from something that's dropped out of my purse. I still remember an interview I had with Matina Horner, the president of Radcliffe College, when Jonathan was only months old—and I was still carrying spare diapers.

For too many years, she said, women have been encouraged to have a career instead of children. "The big difference now is that the younger women are questioning whether that's right," she told me. "They're getting messages from the generation just before them—the women who are now in their mid-30s, who chose what was essentially the new stereotype of the early '70s. Today that group is beginning to say that it's lonely out there, that the rewards of having a high-paying profession are not as terrific as one might think. . . ."

I'm not much of an authority on high-paying professions, but I do know which rewards mean the most to me. While my work may have its interesting moments, it's the constant interruptions—and the lumps in my purse—that really count. ๑

A Christmas Lesson
Darren Stone

At holiday time when the family gathers from various points of the weather vane, the hilarity of first remeetings and measuring the growth of the tallest and smallest grandsons is followed by a spirit of recollection that comes dancing into our midst. ❧ Grandfather remembers the year when one, who is now a mother but was then herself no taller than the yardstick, stuffed a whole package of marshmallows into her mouth while everyone was occupied in the kitchen. ❧ And great-grandmother relates the story of the sleigh carrying Aunt Hetty and the pumpkin pies getting stuck in a snowdrift so that Uncle Carl had to walk Aunt Hetty and the pies three miles to Bradford Woods. ❧

Usually it is after gift-opening, when the whirlwind of ribbons has been rewound for another season of wrappings, and the children's toys, a cardboard box for each, with name, have been put to bed with them, that we get around to remembering gifts which other years have brought. Yet no matter what anyone pulls from his sleeve of memory, the story of my piano tops them all for everyone, and must be repeated.

I remember two pianos.

Perhaps we did have the first one, the great seven-foot grand, at the old rented house. I don't remember hearing it there at all, probably because I was then too involved in the motion of roller skates and bicycles to be still long enough to listen.

But when we moved to our new house on Old English Road the piano, and music, suddenly became very real and very necessary.

125

We had several acres of woods and farmlands around us; it was the first time we had lived away from house-to-house lots and corner drug stores. At first it was birds which I noticed. I would run in to mother waving my description like a flag for her to recognize. "You must have seen an oriole," she might say, "and this morning I heard a thrush singing from the beech tree by the garden. I suppose she is getting ready to nest."

So I became aware that my mother always had time to listen for the song of a bird, to pause as she was weeding the garden and note the warmth of the sun, the slant of a cloud slicing across the blue width of sky.

One evening, walking up the cinder road alone, I heard music. It was an evening full of sunset. The trees seemed to be floating in that orange-fuchsia blend of color behind color, tone on tone. Then I realized the music must be from our house, and our piano.

"Mother, is that you?" I clattered into the house. "I didn't know you could play that way. Why didn't you tell me? It's beautiful."

Mother laughed quietly. "Why, this is MacDowell's *Woodland Sketches*. I've played them ever so often. Maybe they sound better when you're outside listening in. Let me play this one for you; it's called *In Deep Woods*."

It was as though I had never before heard my mother play. The sound of music was a discovery, and with it came a surge of respect and admiration for my mother, my very own mother, who could suddenly make a piano sing so magnificently.

In a week I was taking piano lessons. As a student I was rather sporadic. Sometimes in a fit of determination and devotion I would practice for hours and leap ahead in my lessons so that Mr. Peters began to hope my enthusiasm just might be kindled into ability. But there were some weeks when I sheepishly crept into the studio admitting at once, "I haven't done a bit of practicing."

Still my wondering affection for mother's rippling Liszt, proficient scales and rollicking improvisations grew and grew. Many evenings I would fold myself around our leather hassock in front of the snapping cherry logs in the fireplace, and listen and gaze in deep contentment until the clock struck nine and it was time for a chapter from *Rolf in the Woods* and then to bed.

It seemed too soon after I had discovered the sound and feeling of music, and after my first piano recital was pronounced by Mr. Peters to be "Not too bad after all, not too bad," that my father told us we were moving to another city.

We were accustomed to moving and to new schools, and we rather looked forward to changes. It was a natural component of our family life. But this time, for me, and I was sure for my mother, there was a sadness in our move. For we could not take the piano with us.

"Not take the piano!" I resounded at the dinner table. "Why not? You can't just leave the piano here. It's part of our family. Mother has to have her piano, how else can we have music?"

But the sounding board was cracked and the piano was not worth the cost of moving one thousand miles. And so we settled in the new city in a two-bedroom apartment, piano-less and, for my part, feeling as if part of our family was missing.

Father bought mother a record player. We heard Rubinstein playing Rachmaninoff and Toscanini conducting Beethoven, and it was a new and enriching experience with music. Still I constantly thought of having a piano, as much for myself as for mother. The more I learned about music, the more concerts I went to at the Academy of Music, the more I wanted to touch the notes with my own fingers. "Perhaps we'll move to a house soon, and then we could have a piano again," mother would smile.

"But I want to take lessons *now*. I'm almost through high school (I was a sophomore). And you should have a piano, mother. I mean, anyone who can play the way you do . . ."

Finally I gathered my courage and confided to father how very much mother and I wanted a piano. "For two years now, we've been starving around; I mean, daddy, playing the piano is the most important thing mother can do, and I know I can learn much faster now. In fact—if we can't have a piano for Christmas, then I don't want anything else. I want a piano or nothing."

It was not usual for one of us children to speak in so demanding a tone, and I was quite surprised at myself. Yet my feeling remained very firm.

I have only one recollection of that Christmas morning; it was the frigid moment when I realized, without any doubt, that there were no presents, none at all, under the tree for me. I had worked hard making a few items; potholders and aprons and notebooks for mother, a carved box and enormous painted tray for father, and something I've forgotten about for my brother. But for me there was not even a handkerchief from Grandmother under the tree.

"You told me how you wanted it, honey," father said. "Don't ever deliver an ultimatum like that unless you mean it."

127

"I did mean it. I didn't expect anything," I choked out, and picked up a book and buried my eyes in a maze of print.

I cannot imagine how any of us got through that day; fortunately there were no guests or relatives. Mother, of course, agreed with father that the lesson I had to learn was a valuable one, but how she must have felt my disappointment too.

The day following I went to visit a friend for the morning. It was a clear sun-sparkling day; the snow a clean eight inches on the ground reflected cheer as even Christmas in a city must. Returning home I opened the porch door entering the dining room and quietly greeted mother and father who were looking too intently out of the kitchen window. Proceeding into the living room I was instantly and completely stunned; across the room was a gigantic taffeta red bow perched on the keyboard of a magnificent oversized spinet piano.

"Merry Christmas," mother chimed in with father's shouted greeting. I went to the piano and sat on the bench and put one finger down on middle C; then yesterday's tears began to fall all over the red taffeta bow. Poor mother cried too, and father had to leave the room.

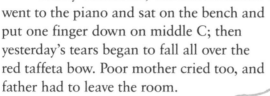

It was the most wonderful, most memorable, most instructive Christmas gift I could then, or even now, imagine; which for all of us extended the joy of that giving far into the several years which followed. ☙

A FAREWELL GIFT
Jim Comstock

Today I wrapped an old dingy, flexible Bible and took it to the post office and mailed it to my daughter in college. ❧ If the saying that "late is better than never" is true, then I have done a good thing. ❧ But I am not sure. ❧

Let me tell you the story. My wife and I had just returned from the 150-mile trip from the college. It was late at night and we were tired. We had left early that morning with our daughter, who had been accepted by the college. Her tuition and her dorm bills and other fees had been sent in previously. She was too excited by the change to need us further, and we drove back home without her. It was the first time in our lives that our daughter had been gone for any length of time. We went to bed, wondering how other people had stood it.

In bed I thought things over. I began to think of the time I went to college. There were a lot of close parallels between my daughter and me. My father had taken me to college, too. That was a good 22 years ago. There were some differences in the mode of transportation. My father and I rode up front in the farm truck. In the back was the trunk that I had pitched hay for that summer. My mother wasn't along because she had to stay behind and keep the cattle from jumping over the fences and getting into the crops. I, the fourth in a line of brothers, was the first to go away to college. And there were brothers and sisters beyond me to use up shoes and to consume groceries. So we went in the truck, my mother cried and I cried, but after we were out of sight of the farm the new changes made me feel jelly-like all over and I was scared.

The truck was slow and my father wasn't used to highways with oncoming cars and people who wanted to pass us and I was glad. I didn't want to get to the city too soon.

129

It was, of course, different with my daughter. We had taken her down during the summer just so she could see the school. On this particular day we stopped at a classy roadside place and ordered fried chicken. In bed I remembered how my father and I had stopped by a little stream of water and ate the sandwiches my mother had prepared. And in bed I relived my daughter's day. We toured the town for a while and then we went to the dormitory and my wife went in and talked with the housemother for a while. When she came back she was wiping her eyes with a handkerchief and it wasn't until we were passing through the next town that my wife remarked something about the weather and discovered that our daughter had forgotten to take out the portable radio and record player. I told her that she should have put it in the trunk with the other things, not in the back seat.

And soon we were home with the long trip behind us and a new kind of loneliness before us and now I was in bed just thinking about my daughter's first trip to college and mine and the score of years between. I heard a little sob beside me and I knew that my wife was thinking about the same thing.

My father didn't let me out at the dormitory. We looked into living conditions in college during the summer, and everybody advised me to get a room in a private home. It was cheaper, and besides if a student wanted to work his way "through," he would have a better chance. Dorms and fraternity houses weren't for me. But I didn't have a room. I had to find one. My father told me that we'd leave my trunk at a filling station and I could come for it the next day after I had found a place to stay. We found the station and we toured the town a little, but the traffic confused him a bit, and I told him that maybe I had better go on my own. I opened the door and I had that awful feeling that a body has when he takes his first swim in the spring and he knows the water is too cold but he just must be brave. And I stepped out onto the street. The water was cold, awfully cold.

I shook hands with my father and for a long, haunting moment he looked straight ahead and didn't say a word. I knew that he was going to make a speech. But it turned out to be very brief. "There is nothing that I can tell you," he said. "I never went to college and none of your brothers went to college. So I can't tell you nothing. I can't say don't do this and for you to do that, because everything is different and I don't know what is going to come up. I can't help you much with money either, but I think things will work out."

He gave me a brand new check book. "If things get pushing, write a little check. But when you write the check, send me a letter and let me know how much. There are some things we can always sell." The mind flits in memory and I recalled the check book and how it was used. In four years all the checks I wrote were less than a thousand dollars. My jobs with the wholesale grocery company, reading to the blind student, chauffering the rich lady, janitoring at the library, sitting with the professors' kids filled in the financial gaps.

I gave my daughter a check book, too. At the end of the first nine months, I know the total will be around $2,000. That is in keeping with the American plan. Kids mustn't have it tough the way the parents did.

"I can't give you any advice. There is no need to. You know what you want to be and they'll tell you what to take. When you get a job, be sure it's honest and work hard." I knew then that it was over almost—that soon I would be myself alone in the big town and I would be missing furrowed ground, cool breezes, and a life where your thinking was done for you. Then my dad reached down beside his seat and brought out that old dingy Bible that he had read so often, and the one he used when he wanted to look something up in a friendly argument with one of the neighbors. I knew it was his favorite and I knew he would miss it. I knew, though, that I must take it.

He didn't say read this every morning. He just said, "This can help you if you will let it." Did it help? I don't know. I got through college without being a burden on the family. I have had a good earning capacity since then. When I finished school, I took the Bible back to my father. But he said he wanted me to keep it. And now in bed and too late, I remember what he said at that time.

"You will have a kid in school. Let the first one take that Bible along," he said.

Now, too late I remember. It would have been so nice to have given it to her, when she, too, got out of the car. But I didn't. Things are different. I was prosperous and my father wasn't. I had gone places. I could give my daughter everything. My father could only give me a battered, old Bible. I was able to give my daughter what she needed . . .

Or, had I? I don't really believe now that I gave her one half as much as my father gave me. So this morning I wrapped that book up and sent it to her. I wrote a note. "This can help you," I said, "if you will let it." ☙

Americans In Paris, or, Are We Having Fun Yet?

Hilary DeVries

I went, I suppose, because it was Paris, and who ever turned down Paris even if it meant going with Mom and Dad? 🐦 Even if it meant going with Mom and Dad, two sisters and a brother-in-law. 🐦

I mean, I was over 30. I had already done France as a foreign exchange student, which was like doing Bergdorf's as a bag lady. I had even managed a business trip when my life later attained a certain yuppie quotient. But I had never done Paris the right way—with a friend and with a tabula rasa for a credit card balance.

"Paris? In April? How fabulous!" friends gushed at my impending travels. So great was their enthusiasm, nay envy, that I couldn't bear to bring up what was rapidly becoming the trip's most salient fact: I was going to Paris as an au pair to my parents—two English-only speakers whose idea of a vacation was the annual car tour of the Great American West.

On this Parisian foray, I was elected tour guide by virtue of my linguistic prowess, a facility that was, truth to tell, about as de facto as you could get. My dad had only left America to attend the Korean war and mom had exhausted her quiche and croissant vocabulary some magazine subscriptions ago.

Plus, I must confess, they bribed me: free food and lodging for the entire 10 days if I came along as translator-in-residence. The Paris dream vacation would have to wait. Three weeks to the day, I was barreling down the autoroute in a rented Renault, squashed between siblings and could you get that Filofax out of my ribs and on your side of the car? *Plus ça change,* I thought.

It wasn't that Paris got the best of us right away. No, the daylong drive from Amsterdam to Paris was as merry as any French 101. Cries of "What's the word for . . ." and "How do you say . . ." filled the car, barely straining my Cook's tour credibility.

Besides, I was feeling real warmth for our intrepid group—a flush of camaraderie that was compounded whenever my dad snapped his credit card to a counter and waved off my feeble attempts to help out with the tip. Perhaps plus ca *did* change.

But our first night in Paris found our conjured bonhomie beginning to crack. It's tempting to blame transatlantic travel arrangements and Parisian hoteliers—"*Non, non, monsieur,* we nevair received a deposit"—for laying to waste our Emily Post politeness. It's even more tempting to blame a too-long tradition of those family car trips. But it was most tempting to blame Paris itself—its silken sophistication, its icy populace, its confounded language.

All heads swiveled in my direction at the first sign of trouble at the registration desk. I was beckoned to the tribunal. Everyone smiled expectantly and Dad looked as if he had just played his trump card. I smiled wanly, unclenched the credit card from his hand, and plunged in. As it turned out, laws of economics mattered far more than my rusty command of the tongue. Dad's command of an impressive credit card was what ultimately held sway.

Still, we didn't get rooms overlooking the courtyard. And my ability to defend the group on foreign soil was shown to be a sham. Everyone was thrown on his own resources—tried and true methods of Getting What You Want When You Want It.

For example: One sister refused to remove her Walkman. Ever. She toured Versailles to the accompaniment of Parisian disc jockeys and dismissed Louis XIV as having a "haircut that predates Mötley Crüe." Another sister, the Los Angeles one, asserted her independence by declining to eat anything made with butter, salt, or heavy cream. Her husband, the California native, spent the week bemoaning Paris's dearth of Mexican food and car dealerships.

"Just because it's France doesn't mean I have to love it," he said, giving Notre Dame a quick once-over before heading off for some nachos or '87 Citroëns, whichever came first. Dad was busy rejecting any bistro not featuring oversize hot fudge sundaes, while Mom maintained that travel was a leisure activity and vetoed any outing that didn't include a taxi or other wheeled transport.

I, for no other reason than lack of alternatives, gamely clung to my schoolgirl French as our family's last hope. After all, I did speak enough to get into a museum, hail a cab, and buy things in better department stores. As a result, wherever I went, at least one family member was sure to follow. The Walkman sister accompanied me to the Musée D'Orsay. The California twins came along on the Left Bank shopping expedition. Mom and Dad rallied for the taxi ride to Montmartre.

Unfortunately, my pidgin French simply buckled in the face of what was rapidly becoming our Waterloo—the We-Are-Not-Amused garçons encountered at every meal. Let's just say we began to eat a lot of what was pictured on menus. Which also tells you a lot about the restaurants we frequented.

After four days of room service and McDonald's, we did the only sensible thing—we fled.

As the gray spires of Paris yielded to the verdant rusticity of Normandy, we visibly relaxed. The man who had unearthed those hidden Colorado treasures years ago was back in charge. He had booked us into a cháteau that took tourists on just this kind of emergency basis. I couldn't have been happier.

Le Moulin de Connelles turned out to be an enormous half-timbered mansion in, oh who cared where, just so long as it wasn't Paris. And the landlady's welcome—a full flinging open of French doors and a torrent of accented but comprehensible English—so emboldened us that we booked a table for dinner.

The meal went swimmingly. With the murmur of French country voices all around us and the candlelight flickering across our faces, we regained our footing. Dad was recovering the gloss of the American Express cardholder. Mom was purring with the thought of several days' drive to come. Even the California kids gave in to the *ris-de-veau* glistening under a butter-rich Bordelaise. But it was the Walkman sister, now minus the earphones, who really put the starch back in our spine.

During the cheese and nut course she inserted a walnut in her nutcracker and began to lip-sync the half-opened shell to the tune of "Gimme Shelter." She was just rounding the second verse when the nut exploded, sending shells sailing across the white linen hush of the dining room. The We-Are-Not-Amused swiveled in our direction. Too late. For once, we were too amused by our own family faux pas to be cowed by stern gazes and muttered criticism: "*Les Americains* nevair know how to behave."

They were right. We couldn't and it was great. ☙

LETTER TO MY FATHER
David Mazel

Dear Papa: Thank you for the beautiful book you gave me for my birthday. ᔓ It's right here beside me now, as I write. ᔓ Thank you especially for the dedication, "For my son, the writer. Love, Papa." ᔓ

There's something else I want to thank you for, too. It's not tangible like a book, but it's just as real, just as vital, in my life. It's the way you have always accepted me, embraced me; the way you have let me grow up to find for myself the best combination of survival and happiness possible.

You never made me feel that I would disappoint you if I didn't become something prestigious in the business world, like an executive, or a lawyer, or a CPA.

Remember Rubin, one of the fellows I palled around with in college? He became a CPA. I'll never forget how he had a pencil propped behind each ear for rapid entries into any number of ledgers he always had with him. Once, he and I stopped to look at some daisies. I winked at them because I could have sworn they winked at me first.

But Rubin, he gave them a long, careful look, as if he were weighing their credits against their debits. He must have known from the beginning that he wanted to be a CPA.

And remember Springel and Hartman? They were on the debating team. And now they're lawyers. They know how to open—and I don't mean burgle—the safes of the world.

And me, what do I do? I make a living by translating works in other languages into English. I lead words and silences from other lands, other worlds, over the mountains to safety and delight in our land, our world. I am their guide. And at night, a look of wistful purpose on my face, I do my own writing. Sometimes I wish I could write in another language and then translate it into English. In that way, if my writing failed, I could blame the translator. But I don't have the temperament to be devious.

Even when I was a child, I wrote. I kept in notebooks an account, every day, of the things I'd seen that helped the world, like trees and the sky—by lifting—and of the things that tried in vain to spoil the world, like long distances and dark stairs—by scaring.

I still have those notebooks, Papa. Most of the penciled, printed words have resisted time's invisible eraser, and I can still make out the doodles I sometimes drew in the margins, where a whimsical part of me always felt free. When I reread the old notebooks I know that remembering and discovering are one and the same.

Life for me has not been an upward thing, but a thing of ups and downs in approximately equal measure. I don't have every day something sensational to report about my progress. And often I wonder if fulfillment in life is necessarily tied to a change for the better.

A few days ago my rabbi asked me how things were going, and I answered, "Things are going all right, but it wouldn't hurt if they went a little better." Raising his formidable eyebrows, he said, "And how do you *know* it wouldn't hurt?"

Earlier today I was looking at some old photographs, gazing into them as into a lost world. There was one of me as a child, a wisp of a boy, standing next to a whopper of a man, my towering father. I looked like a little bush growing alongside a giant oak, secretly proud that we shared the same sunlight. You were looking down at your shy-eyed son with an expression that said, "Every child brings his own blessing into the world. And this one, what will be his?"

Papa, I think I'll go out for a walk, and mail this letter at the trusty box on the corner. It was cold earlier, and drizzly. A drizzle like a dim snow. Soon there will be real snow. The sky's laundry, blown down from the clotheslines strung between the stars, will be hanging everywhere.

Blessed is the son who writes to his father. Blessed is the father who keeps the letters in an honored place. Blessed is love, stronger than death. ☙

Split Green Vases
Alma Roberts Giordan

His given name was Warren. ⋐ He was folding his tent and moving on to greener pastures, he told Bob, and: "A person who transfers jobs the way I do can't be trailing too many belongings." ⋐ So he asked Bob if we could use another bookcase. ⋐ He didn't want to sell it—how could he put a price on something he'd made himself, with care and love and uncounted hours of pure pleasure? ⋐

So we invited him to a farewell dinner and Warren borrowed a truck to deliver the bookcase. He hadn't intended it to contain just books, he explained, though that would be our sole objective. It was five feet wide and three tall, with doors at either end featuring hand-turned knobs. The entire top shelf was free, but the two beneath it were curtailed, necessarily, by the shelves within those doors. It is still in Bob's den after some 20 years, filled with books and papers and other paraphernalia peculiar to an artist's bailiwick.

But Warren brought something else when he came to dinner. Shyly he presented a green vase, triangular in shape—yes, it had three sharply defined sides to it. Toward the bottom was a colorful mallard duck, with purple-tinged wings spread as in flight—one tip presenting a precarious breakoff point. Amber cattails, raised on the surface, provided a background for the bird. (The potential was realized, one wing tip has been twice repaired.)

The vase, our friend said, was one of a pair. He meant to keep the mate in memory of Bob's kindness to him when he first came to work at the engineering plant. Wherever he traveled in the future, he would take his vase along. And he hoped we would treasure ours, remembering him whenever we used it. It might have been a maudlin moment, but it wasn't. Warren was a

137

no-nonsense person, and Bob and I filled in the span with sincere admiration.

Down the ensuing years we made ultimate use of Warren's bookcase. But the lovely ceramic vase, with its flying mallard drake, wasn't something to use every day. (After Bob mended the tip I was more careful, using the vase less frequently.) I preferred glass vases that showed the interesting stems of flowers. And Warren's vase usually was a bit largish—over a foot tall, and the duck's wingspread inches beyond the base.

Eventually, the green container was relegated to a small cabinet over the refrigerator, where seldom-used treasures were stored; it was practically inaccessible to me unless I stood on something. Even then it was all I could do to reach across and into that shelf. Dust, which has never been on my list of priorities, was gathering up there. However, when Bob retrieved the crystal bowl in which I always put Christmas beads, he also knew. And promised to help me clean the cabinet.

So out came Warren's vase again, in need of a washing, as were all the other rarely used items up there. When the pale green gleamed and the mallard seemed eager to fly once more, I didn't have the heart to consign it to the rear of that remote shelf so soon again. So I went out and trimmed the yew (which was growing into a tree instead of a bush, anyway). I placed half a dozen long whips in Warren's vase on one side of the hearth, and when it came to trimming the house for Christmas, decorated them with tiny angels. Long after the tree came down and all the other holiday artifacts were put away, the vase with its dark, living branches remained in place. Whenever I thought it really must be time to dispose of them, I was checked by their dark vivacity. And then, one January day, when the snow lay a foot deep over the whole world outside, the branches began to display light green tips. They were actually sprouting. By February they were still full of promise, and by April those stiff branches had long white *roots*. They were drinking up water at a great clip—and the chartreuse sprouts had extended with a vengeance.

So when the season seemed more appropriate, I dug a hole in the backyard and planted one more yew—putting all the branches in together. Finally, I washed the vase and put it away. Not on that high, inaccessible shelf over the refrigerator this time, but in one of those side-cabinets of Warren's bookcase. The repaired tip had come off, and Bob had restored it again—so the vase isn't perfect. But then, neither are we.

And Warren—wherever he is—may still have his matching vase, and maybe he still uses it on occasion, and remembers us when he does. 🖎

138

SOMETHING SHE MAY NOT HAVE KNOWN BEFORE
Patience M. Canham

I'd been aware of Susie for some time. ✒ She was a wriggling presence in any supposedly straight line—the shrillest protester in a playground skirmish. ✒

She was seven by the time she became my responsibility every school day. A skinny, unheeding child with perm-frizzed hair. For quite a while neither was any help to the other. Susie broke the crayons, scribbled in other people's books—her own she lost—left scissors in the clay, and joined in any quarrel she hadn't already started. I reasoned, pleaded, scolded, became shrill myself. Susie wept—and did it all again.

Then one morning I had a break. Susie spilled blue paint down her dress. Of course I should have noticed before it happened. But I was immersed in a group of readers; and she wasn't supposed to be anywhere near the paint. I sighed, made the obvious point, cleaned her up as best I could, told her to tell her mother the paint would wash out, and returned to my queue of waving books.

Ten minutes later, Susie was crying. This puzzled me. She didn't have that long a crying cycle—ten seconds or as soon as my eye was off her was the usual pattern. I'd been much crosser with no effect, so why the tears now? Ignoring aggrieved noises—"Miss, hear me. It's my turn next"—I wandered over to where she was sitting. The tears were real. "Me dress is spoiled, Miss. I'll catch out with me Dad."

This was standard rhetoric. Mothers in that district had to take turns at the wash house, and Susie's dress should have lasted at least a week. Dad—if there was one—was used as a kind of back-up threat. Most likely he wouldn't take any notice. But something—call it that which steers teachers in their fumbling reach for wisdom—something kept me sitting there, my arm round Susie. (I'd learned by then that an affectionate arm is worth a hundred words.)

I reviewed my scanty knowledge. There were several younger children in the family. I'd seen them with the mother—immaculate for that area, but quite unable to cope with Susie. Yet a few spots of paint: she could manage that, I'd have thought. "Me Dad" I'd never seen.

Then I remembered. He only claimed the younger children; Susie was the result of some earlier encounter the mother had had. Perhaps there might be reason for the tears.

It was easy to fix. The paint really did wash out. By hometime that afternoon the dress was clean and pressed. Susie was ecstatic. "You're my friend, aren't you?" Her hug nearly strangled.

After that my little gadfly became my ally. Always ready to catch my eye, eager to help pick up, she would shush the other children into place. I felt small. I often did in face of such generous response to so little.

Some months later Susie was lingering after school.

"Next year I won't be in your class, will I?"

"No, Susie, you'll be in Miss B's."

"Can I come and see you then? Can I help at playtime? Will you still be my friend?"

Her hold on good was very uncertain. It was only March, and she was worrying about September. And I knew what she hadn't yet been told. I'd been promoted and was leaving that school after Easter. If her good was wrapped up in me, there was even less than she thought.

I ached as I walked up the street that evening. Had I done wrong? Should I not have let her get so fond? Could I have prevented it? She received no favors. She was one among fifty kids, and knew it. Besides, I had plenty of other special relationships that had developed out of need. Perhaps I was hurting them all.

That night there was a lecture on education. I didn't feel like it, but I'd signed up, and so I went. Things began badly. The speaker was wearing a perfectly dreadful purple dress and simpered through the introduction. I nearly went home.

But it soon became obvious that this was no theory flung across a gulf. The speaker had been in the classroom. She remembered what it was like. And she still cared. She'd even agonized about the same thing that was troubling me. Her Susie was a boy, but the problem was the same. A bond had formed and then she had to change schools. Was it wrong to show love? Especially to the unloved when one couldn't be a permanency for them?

She had taken her anguish to Susan Isaacs, that wise educationalist.

As I remember it, Susan Isaacs had said: "No, it isn't wrong. You have shown him what love is, and he will always recognize it when he meets it again. And you have proved to him that *he* is lovable—something he may not have known before."

This all happened years ago. Other Susies have come and gone. But those words are still reassuring. Once love is felt, it doesn't vanish with the person. 🐚

THE WORLD
WE SHARE

OFF THE PLANE AND INTO OUR ARMS
Susan Tiberghien

Daniel was two years old when he arrived. ❧ We were waiting at the airport. ❧ We were waiting and wondering if he would ever really be there, if he would ever really come home with us. ❧

One year earlier, we had written to a distant relative, a Benedictine sister, living in Saigon. We asked her if she knew of a war orphan who needed a family. We were living in Geneva, in a new house of our own. We had room for another child.

I still remember receiving her answer. As I tore open the envelope, a photo fell out, a small photo of one-year-old Daniel. He looked the size of a newborn baby, with a very large head and very dark, large eyes. He was sitting in a little straw chair, leaning to one side, as if he would topple right out.

The Benedictine sister wrote that the mother had handed her the under-nourished baby before she moved on with a group of Cambodian refugees. The father, an American soldier, had disappeared. The very day my letter arrived, the sister had received the first satisfactory bill of health for Daniel after months of intensive medical care.

We then spoke to each one of our children about welcoming a new baby into our family. Peter, the oldest, was 13. He was in the kitchen looking at the world map on the wall, when I mentioned it for the first time. He turned around and looked at me in surprise. "Mom, would you believe it?" he said. "I was just looking at the map and wondering if we could do something like that."

The next two are girls. They were then 11 and 9. "Another baby?" they asked and shouted together. "Why not two? Please, Mom and Dad, can't we have two? Each of us can take care of one." They both kept asking for still another baby for a long time. "There's still room for a seventh, please?"

The two youngest, a boy and a girl, aged 6 and 3, didn't care where their new little brother was coming from. They'd be the closest. They were the littlest. And when his teacher asked six-year-old Christopher what it felt like to be waiting for . . . , she hesitated. She didn't know what to call him.

"You mean my little brother?" said Christopher, without a moment of hesitation. "It feels great."

So we waited together. Each new letter we shared. At Christmas time we received a second photo. Daniel was standing up this time. We recognized the same little straw chair. He was holding on to it with both hands. We put the photo in the middle of the Christmas tree. Daniel was to be the family's forever gift.

The two youngest children moved in together, leaving the smaller bedroom for their little brother. We got down the white wooden crib from the attic and repainted it. Each child picked out one of his favorite stuffed animals —one pink bunny, one spotted leopard, and three worn-out brown and white teddy bears—and put them on Daniel's bed. I went through our cartons of baby clothes, remembering when each of the others was still a baby.

All we knew about Daniel was that he was staying in an orphanage on the outskirts of Saigon, with hundreds of other refugee children. I never asked about anything else, such as what he ate, where he slept, how he played, what he spoke. I just thought that once he was in our family, he would grow up with his brothers and sisters.

It took us six months to complete the legal papers for the adoption. The judgment was made in January. Then we had to obtain a visa for Daniel to enter Switzerland. The Swiss authorities questioned and requestioned us.

"Madame, have you thought this all through?" they asked.

"Yes, I have," I answered.

"Then if you really want another child, why don't you have one of your own? We already have many foreigners in Switzerland."

We explained and reexplained. We said that we ourselves were foreigners and that Daniel was one of us.

Finally everything was ready. Daniel had a Vietnamese passport and a Swiss visa. He could come to us. Now we had to find transportation. This was back in early 1974. The Viet Cong were encircling Saigon. Very few planes were coming in or going out. We learned that Air France each week was flying a group of orphans to Paris. We put Daniel on the list.

Week after week we waited, thinking next time it would be his turn.

145

Each day the children came home from school, hoping their little brother would be on his way. And still there was no news.

When the phone rang, I knew it was my husband calling from Paris.

"I have news," he said.

"Yes?"

"The plane has been delayed. It had to stop for repairs...." What else did he say? I don't remember. Only that he would call back as soon as he learned something more.

The children came home for lunch. They were excused for the afternoon and expecting to pile into the car and drive to the airport.

"What do you mean, the plane had to stop somewhere?"

"What happened?"

"And Daniel, where is he?"

I answered as best I could and assured them that their little brother would soon be with us.

I couldn't send them back to school, each child alone in his class, wondering all the time whether Daniel would ever arrive. We stayed together and tried to pass the time. When the phone rang again, the children let me answer.

"The plane will land in less than an hour," my husband said. "That means I should be able to make the 5 o'clock flight to Geneva."

"With Daniel?"

"With Daniel."

Somehow the last hours passed. Somehow we got into the car and drove to the airport. Was it my heart, or was it really the car, skidding all the way? I knew the streets well, yet everything looked different. I was going into unchartered land.

We hurried into the terminal. The flight from Paris had just landed. We crowded behind the wide glass window and looked at the far end of the luggage hall, where the passengers were arriving. The five children got themselves up front and pressed their searching faces flat against the glass. I stood behind. I was suddenly afraid.

Then I saw my husband. He was taller than the other passengers. He was carrying our Daniel in his arms.

"I see him! Look, I see Daddy!" shouted the oldest daughter.

"He's there. He's there!"

"Where, where is he?" "There. And he's got Daniel!"

146

"Mom, do you see them?" asked my oldest son. He turned and looked at me. I was crying.

We went to the arrival gate. My husband and Daniel were among the first. They had no baggage, just each other, father and son. My husband waved to us and put Daniel down, trying to stand him on his feet. But Daniel didn't know how to stand up alone. He fell forward on the floor. The straw chair, the one he was holding on to in the photos, had remained in Saigon.

We took him in our arms and carried him home. ☙

WINTER IN AFRICA
Paul Theroux

Ptolemy guessed that there was snow on the equator but it was not until 1848 that Johann Rebmann actually saw it. ❧ Rebmann noted in his diary that it was a "dazzling white cloud" on Mount Kilimanjaro; his guide told him that it was called "beredi," cold. ❧

The idea of snow on the equator was ridiculed even after Rebmann's discovery and it was some time before it was a proven fact. Late in the 19th century it was discovered that the snow on the Ruwenzoris (what Ptolemy had called "the Mountains of the Moon") provided the water which was one of the sources of the River Nile.

Ptolemy was more realistic about these matters than most people were, or are. It can be very cold in Africa.

In the tiny country of Malawi the winter is severe, though paradoxical, and the inhabitants of this country are both eager and hesitant to greet it. May, June and July, the cold months, are also the harvest months. This is the season when the village silos—huge baskets on legs—are filled to the brim with corn, the staple food of the Malawian. The oranges and tangerines are ripe; the second bean crop, the tobacco and tea are all being harvested and auctioned. This is the season when there are jobs, a season of feasting in the cold.

On the plateaus the cold wet winds sting the countryside with a mixture of fog and rain. These winds whip sideways against the face, tear and flatten the elephant grass and yank swatches of thatch from the roofs of the mud houses. Yet one rarely hears complaints about this cold season—food is a great blessing in a poor country. Few mention the discomfort and perhaps this is the reason no one has popularized the African winter.

As an English teacher I can tell the season by the changing conditions of the exercise books. In the rainy season, spring, the books are damp, the ink has run, and the point of the red grading pencil gets soggy and usually breaks. Winter arrives in Malawi and the students' exercise books are charred at the edges, the stack of books reeks of woodsmoke and dampness. Sometimes moons of candlewax appear on the pages.

This is circumstantial evidence of the season, of the conditions under which those essays on truth or "Treasure Island" are written. One corrects the compositions and a small room materializes. The room is either of cement or mud and has a grass roof; in the corner of the room a boy squints at an exercise book under the feeble flickering light of a candle or the low flame of a wick stuck in a dish of kerosene. The kerosene lamp gives off a deep yellow light and fills the room with thick smoke. In the center of the room a pile of smoldering coals in a pit warms the student and his sleeping family.

In the townships just outside the large cities of Central Africa—Salisbury, Blantyre, Lusaka—winter can be dismal. It is not a time of harvest since the persons that live in the townships in those millions of cement sheds, are civil servants, mechanics, shopgirls and students. Even if there were time to plant and care for a garden there would be no space for the garden. The townships stretch row on row, symmetrical treeless towns, long files of tiny white one-room or two-room houses. Rusting signboards appear at intervals on the dirt roads that run in a grid in the townships. And early in the morning, before dawn, a stream of people winds its way among the unnamed roads. The school children, many without shoes, run stifflegged in the cold; the girls march in clumps, hugging themselves in their long cloths.

At the assembly, held outside the school in the morning, the national anthem is sung by three hundred shivering children. Their teeth chatter and they hop up and down between choruses to keep warm. If anyone owns shoes this is the season for them. The leather shoes are patched, sewn, and some are in shreds; some wear plastic shoes—made in Rhodesia or Japan—which are uncomfortable and very little protection against the cold.

In class the wind sounds like someone crawling slowly around the corrugated roof, a heavy man trying to break through the tin. After school there is a vigorous soccer game. No one dares to stand still, the players dash about the field—a ballet on the grass with a backdrop of trees tossing in the fog.

In the villages after supper the people can be seen crouching around fires to warm themselves. A student of mine once suggested that independence in Malawi came at a perfect time of the year. He said the day of independence

149

comes in July, with winter at its coldest, and the people who would naturally be together around the fires would have a good opportunity to discuss the meaning of the freedom they had won for themselves.

There are places in Africa that are colder than Malawi. In Basutoland, where the national costume is the blanket, the people can expect snow, sometimes two or three feet of it. Freezing winds sweep across the Karoo tableland of South Africa, batter the Great Rift escarpments in Kenya and Uganda.

Winter in Africa? Yes, just as sure as there is snow on the equator. Winter in Africa is much more than a word. And though one may not associate cold with this continent it is there as conspicuous and intense as the heat, and perhaps as unpublicized as the peace that also exists in Africa. 🐂

MERCY'S GREETING
Bunny McBride

Mid winter. 🐘 New York City. 🐘 The sky was dark and hard. 🐘 Sharp cold sliced through the seams of my thick woolen coat, weaseled through the pores of my leather gloves. 🐘 I'd spent the evening in the library, and now, racing against the late night cold, pressing bookbag to chest, I ran to board the subway. 🐘 The Red Line: it stretched from Harlem, through the city's Upper West Side where I went to school, and down toward the Lower East Side where I lived. 🐘 As I sat down, my eyes started to burn with the sudden switch from night's cold cutting wind to the train's warm, stale air. 🐘

Like all New York's subways, the Red Line usually carries a thousand themes of humanity. But not tonight. Tonight it carried only one man and me.

The train had screeched through half a dozen stops before I noticed him in a nearby seat. He wore a cumbersome gray-blue coat, ventilated with a dozen holes, belted with rags. Legs sprawled, head bent forward, masses of woolly black hair pressed against one knee. His right arm clutched two bulky bags that sat beside him and cushioned him like kind old ladies. The other arm hung limp between his legs, long thick fingers dangling like weary overweight dancers. Safety pins secured the seams of his green pants—pants that hung short of bare ankles that were swollen with cold, chalked white from the salt and ice of winter streets and sidewalks. Tie shoes, lacking laces and too big in size, encased his sockless feet.

Curiously, I felt empathy more than pity for this survivor who had apparently come to the subway for heat and rest, and who was now, almost contentedly, sucking wisps of warm air into his throat. I wondered what sort of jolt in his life's journey had brought him here. I couldn't see his face, but somehow I recognized him—or recognized in him my own desire to survive the harsher chapters of life. And as I watched him, I marveled at his durability, conscious that the jolts in my life were no doubt less enormous than his.

I don't know how long I stared at him, but suddenly I was aware that the train was approaching my stop. I looked at his pathetic shoes, and then down at my own booted feet, knowing that under those boots was a layer of jeans and under those jeans a double padding of wool socks. Socks never seemed so important as they did at that moment, and I found myself trying to figure out if there was time to remove my boots, yank off my socks, offer them to the man and pull both boots back on before the subway reached my destination. But the conductor hit the brakes, and I, feeling a strange desperation to offer something to this man who had asked for nothing, reached into my coat pocket and retrieved its contents: two dollars. *It's not much,* I thought. But the train was stopping. Hastily I got up, pushed the money deep into one of the man's bags and, apparently unnoticed by him, got off the train. In the days that followed, I occasionally thought about the man, wondering what the face behind all that hair was like, imagined him shuffling through his bag and happening on the money.

When to give, *whether* to give, is a question everyone who lives or visits New York has to contend with, no matter where in that city of contrasts one lives. I know one fellow who, each morning, tore the want ads out of the paper and stuffed them into his breast pocket. When approached for handouts on his way to or from work, he would invite the solicitor to a café and offer to help them hunt the ads for work. Most turned down his offer. Occasionally someone accepted. Once someone even got a job. But mostly I've seen myself and others passing by extended hands like priests and Levites on the road to Jericho.

One builds up defenses in a big city, and develops self-survival blinders that are not easily penetrated. The needs of people can be so desperate, so constant, that one closes her eyes because she imagines that to open them is to be overwhelmed. Once, while walking down Second Avenue in my neighborhood, I saw ahead of me people detouring around something on the sidewalk. When I reached the detour I discovered they were all avoiding a body sprawled on the pavement. I, too, walked around the figure. For the next two blocks and all the way up my apartment steps, I thought of that man. I took off my coat and hung it up, all the while chiding myself with the question, *How much effort would it have taken to hoist the fellow up and sit with him at the corner café over a warm drink?* I put my coat back on, ran down the steps and hurried to the corner where I'd passed the man. But he was gone. Had he pulled himself up? Had someone with more courage and heart than I happen by? My friend with his want ads?

Two weeks after encountering the man who'd been sleeping on the train, I again turned into an Upper West Side subway entrance. Glancing down the stairwell, I spotted a figure crowned with a mass of woolly black hair. He wore a cumbersome gray-blue coat, held together with rags. I called *hello* to that familiar coat, and the man inside it looked up. Somehow the face, not just the clothing, seemed familiar. I skipped down the steps as if an old friend waited for me at the bottom. I walked up to the man and heard myself ask, "Do you need money for the subway?" Somewhat startled, he responded by opening his palm and revealing a handful of small change. "I don't need all of it; I already have 15 cents," he told me. Responding to the strength, as well as the struggle in that outreached hand, I gave him the balance—and he, with that face I somehow knew so well, gave me a smile.

I'd recognized the man, even before I'd seen his face. ᝐ

Diary Of A Veteran Returning To Vietnam
Larry Rottmann

Dallas. 12/20/87 P.M. Shortly after takeoff, flight attendant Leslie Clark, wife of a Vietnam vet, approaches me. 🐚 She says her husband served with the 25th Infantry Division. 🐚 She thanks me for going back—says she wishes her husband would too —she feels it would help him. 🐚 Later, the airplane captain seeks me out. 🐚 He's a pilot who flew jets out of Tan Son Nhut Airport in Saigon in '67-68. 🐚 He says returning is "brave." 🐚 Says he'd like to go back, but never will. 🐚

When I deplane in Los Angeles, both the pilot and Leslie are waiting for me at the door. "Thanks for going back and for understanding," they say. Both are misty-eyed. I'm amazed. The long journey is truly under way at last.

12/28/87 A.M. Seoul. I'm at the window of my downtown hotel. It's 3:06 and I can't sleep. . . . I think I'm frightened, not for my safety, but for something more central, more immediate. I guess I'm afraid of not what I'll learn additionally about Vietnam, but what I might learn anew about myself.

12/30/87 A.M. Bangkok. In just a few hours, I'll be returning to Viet-am. It still doesn't seem real. My mind is seething with images, memories, impressions—so that even though I need to, I cannot sleep, not this night. My apprehension is so powerful, I wonder if it is visible to others. . . .

Even after seeing combat and becoming acquainted with the real horrors of war, I still wasn't fully aware of the immorality of my own participation in it. That knowledge has come to me more slowly over many years. It is not an awareness that leads to personal tranquillity, but is, in fact, a realization that unsettles me profoundly in a part of my heart where I rarely even allow myself to tread.

So terrible are these memories and truths that I've never allowed them to come fully to the surface. I fear I will finally be forced to confront them head-on before this day is over.

I am not ready. I want to call it off. I want to turn back.

12/30/87 P.M. Yen Phu. Sitting on my bed in Room 235 of the Thang Loi (Victory) Hotel, watching the sun sink slowly over Ho Tay Lake, I watch the lights begin to wink on across the water in a small fishing village. . . .

I'm glad to have a private room, for I cannot imagine being forced to share my thoughts and feelings this evening with anyone.

1/9/88 A.M. Da Nang. The waves on China Beach advance and retreat the way wartime memories ebb and eddy around the obstructions of my daily routine back home, repeating over and over the gentle whisper of Ho Chi Minh. "The wheel of life turns without pause . . . . Men and animals rise up reborn."

The waves on China Beach advance and retreat, and I kneel upon the sand and weep the grief I've hoarded for 20 years.

1/10/88 A.M. Highway 1. To get a better feel for the character of Vietnam, I ought to bicycle—or better yet, walk—the length of this road. But that would be difficult, mostly because many Vietnamese have never seen an American. They are fascinated. Curious. Even a bit frightened—not of me or my past connections—but of my strangeness. My skin color. My height. My beard. My clothes.

To stop in any small town, at any time, is to precipitate a near-riot. In minutes, and solely by word of mouth, the news is passed. People of all ages come from all over to look at me, to touch me. It's like being an alien. Everyone wants to see me, to learn about me, but no one knows who I am or what I'm doing in their village.

The kids approach first, shyly but inquisitively. It doesn't take long to make friends with them. I pass out a handful of "superballs" which I have brought along just for this purpose, and soon the balls are bouncing wildly all over the highway. Next come the teen-agers, bolder, and even more curious. Shortly thereafter come the grandmothers, who can be the sweetest and the most fun. Sometimes they pinch me hard just to see if I'm real (I learn to yelp in pain immediately and loud; they like that).

The middle-aged men usually hang way back. Many of them, of course, are former guerrillas, and thus are understandably reluctant to approach. Some feign indifference. But others edge closer, too interested

155

in an old enemy (whom most never met face to face) to resist. Grandfathers are usually the last to arrive but are often the most friendly.

The old men are talkative, and are eager to discuss farming and fishing. Do you grow rice in America? How do you catch fish? I show them a nearly worn-out photo of my son, which is quickly passed from hand to hand. His blond hair and open smile draw "oh's" and "ah's" from the crowd, and an aggressive matchmaker offers me a local girl as a potential wife for Leroy. . . .

But a middle-aged woman on the outside fringe of the crowd reminds me sharply of a former reality by shouting an all too familiar phrase, "Go home GI, go home!"

1/10/88 P.M. Nha Trang. I find it increasingly difficult to sleep on this trip. . . .

I'm having formless dreams, impressions without plot, images without recognition. Things I've seen. Pictures I've taken. All the intense experiences in the last couple of weeks piled on top of that closely hoarded collection of seething memories from the war. My brain and heart are working overtime —overloaded with complicity and good intentions.

I can't keep up with the incoming flood of information. My input is days, weeks, months ahead of my output. But I want more data. I'm hungry for it. I'm dying of thirst for Vietnam. I cannot slake that need.

I need faces and names. I never got to learn who these people were last time. I spent a whole year here before, but I don't remember a single Vietnamese person I knew.

So far I have the names and addresses and photos of 81 people whose hands I've shaken, whose families I've met, whose meals I've eaten, whose kids I've held.

I want to meet these folks. To hold them. Touch them. Smell their life and sweat. I want to know they are alive, especially the children. I need to be reassured that we didn't kill or poison them all. Or destroy their individuality or their collective spirit.

I wallow in the happiness of the children, and am buoyed by their smiles and laughter and sense of life and purpose. A sleeping baby. A pregnant woman. A nursing mother. A young couple holding hands and making "moon eyes." It feels very good to know that Vietnam lives!

1/18/88 P.M. Cu Chi. Sitting on the porch of Nguyen Van Sen's farmhouse, I can see the site where I was stationed 20 years ago. Sen raises sugar cane, wheat, and rice in fields reclaimed from the sprawling 25th

Infantry Division base camp.

For a while, I just wander about the area, lost in thought. I am not unhappy, but reflective. My capacity for remorse has been exhausted. I'm ready, eager, to start thinking ahead. About what I might do in the future regarding Vietnam.

What I'd believed was a bottomless well of grief has dried up. I'm too full now of new names and faces and places and experiences and ideas to have room or time for that old sorrow. Maybe my hosts understood that— expected that—and have arranged the entire visit to conclude this way. On a hopeful note. Or perhaps this reconciliation has been my own personal agenda all along.

1/22/88 P.M. Honolulu. Coming through Customs, the agent (a vet) is astonished to see "Vietnam" visas stamped in my passport.

"You went back?" he asks. "Really?" He's now only going through the motions of examining my bags.

"You went back voluntarily? I hated it. Hated it."

He pauses, lost in thought, then turns up the Viet Cong pith helmet, complete with red star, that I'd traded my Bass Pro Shop hat for. The inspector is stunned.

"Where'd you get this?" he asks, almost in a whisper. I tell him.

"I hated Vietnam," he repeats. "Hated it." He's lost all interest in my luggage now. He looks at me, but doesn't even see me. I wait. Finally, the question comes, hesitatingly. "What's it like, now?"

He asks: Have I been to Da Nang? Did I see the air base? What's the city like? How are the people? Do they hate us? I tell him that most do not.

He's silent for a moment, then says, "If I were them, I would."

Finally, the inspector passes me on through, but as I leave, he calls me back, takes me aside, and asks, "Do you think I could go back sometime?"

2/7/88 P.M. Springfield, Missouri. I've been back for a couple of weeks now, but I'm still having a difficult time readjusting. I'm still back on that journey that, in some basic and profound way, has altered forever who I am.

I know I wasn't ready to come back yet. Part of me remained in Vietnam in 1968, and another (larger) piece of me stayed this time. I've got to go back, and soon.

I've been too busy since I returned to examine whether I've gained any valuable perspective. But last night for the first time ever, I dreamed about Vietnam at peace. 🐾

A Garden Party With Chagall
Norma Lofthouse

It was a charming scene—a few ladies in summer frocks gathered on the lawn to paint and to have tea—a Seurat painting in an English garden, all pastels and dappled sunlight. ❧

But at some point during the course of that long, golden afternoon Chagall arrived, gave Seurat the boot, turned adults upside down into children, and painted the grass a bright blue. It was all because of those rocks I had brought back from the railway house. There was a kind of magic in them, I think.

I had been up to the abandoned railway line the previous week, poking among the rubble of the railwayman's house, wandering along the old track-bed, following the footpaths that bind the Bedfordshire countryside together into a patchwork of farms and villages. I was in a melancholy mood. Our year of living in rural England was turning out to be a lonely experience for me. The village we had chosen to settle in was charming—close to my husband's university and pretty as a post card with its thatched cottages, rose gardens, and broad water meadows. But I found it a terribly shy place, parochial in its habits, and wary of strangers. I longed to chat with folks about rural ways and old days, but I couldn't get beneath the polite smiles and nods.

It was while musing thus in the ruins of the railway house that I spotted some stones lying in a nearby field probably brought to the surface recently by a farmer's plow. They were whimsically shaped things, some round with flattened bottoms, some pyramidal, some smooth and nearly square. In shape they reminded me of the thatched cottages down on the village green, and I took them home.

With some paint from the shop, I painted them to resemble the village cottages, with rosebushes clinging to their walls and wispy gray roofs that looked somewhat like thatch. They were humble, humorous—the kind of love objects a child brings home from kindergarten. I put them on the windowsill to dry and forgot about them.

And then, overnight, as if released from a capped bottle, the village began to unfold. Perhaps it was the English love of things tiny and nursery-like. Perhaps it was my silent exaltation of the small, subtle charms of the village. Whatever the reason, my cottage rocks had managed, in their simple way, to open the door for me a little.

The next day the doorbell rang. Some neighbors stopped to inquire about the little rocks in the window. Had I done them myself? Where had I gotten the idea?

I explained that where I came from, rock-painting was a popular hobby and people were always capturing their houses, their pets, the bugs in their gardens, on stone. It was easy. Everybody did it. It was fun.

The hook went in.

Could we perhaps arrange an afternoon sometime when I could show them how to do it?

Of course we could.

And so the following Thursday I found myself seated in my neighbor's garden surrounded by ladies in summer dresses and card tables laden with field rocks. My neighbor was providing the tea, I was providing the expertise, and the others had brought their own rocks and whatever paints and brushes they could scrounge from their grandchildren's paint sets.

We started gingerly, feeling our way, sitting rather awkwardly at our card tables, talking about the garden and the weather. There was a sense of discomfiture among the women, each one unsure of her talents, of whether or not her work would measure up to that of the others. A little row of white-washed stones grew along the edge of the card tables, stiff and precise, with black windows painted in grids, like jail bars. No charm. No joy. And I had said it would be fun. I was beginning to despair.

But then, at the darkest moment, help arrived. Chagall came, in spirit, bringing with him his brilliant palette and his flying cows and his lovers embracing under starry skies. He came in answer to prayer, and I knew he had arrived when my knee accidentally knocked the leg of the card table and the wet rocks went flying, to land paintside down in the flower bed. I retrieved them and set them right-side up and dirt-smeared on the card table, mumbling apologies. Somebody giggled and stood up quickly, upsetting the

159

cobalt blue onto the grass. It pooled into a circle of intense blue, cupped in the green grass like a mountain lake. We salvaged what we could of the remaining paint and sat down.

But by now the Chagallian spirit had settled over us all. Everyone's work was ruined. Nothing could be perfect anymore. The best we could do would be to tidy things up a bit and have fun. We touched up the damaged rocks with fresh paint, adding a few daubs of pure color here and there among the grass stains to give the illusion of flowers. My neighbor said they were herbs, and showed me how a dormer window fits up under a thatch roof and how wire netting protects the straw from the burrowings of birds and small animals.

Each rock prompted a story. I learned never to stand in the doorway of a thatched cottage in the rain (no eaves) and how the railway engineers used to "accidentally drop" a little coal on the tracks by the railway house during the depression years. I learned about the plans to clean the cobwebs out of the old corn mill and turn it into a craft center and how the old farm buildings down by the river had been fixed up and let to weekend artists and writers from London.

We painted all afternoon, stopping briefly for tea, and then painted again until shadows fell across the lawn and grandfathers came back from the allotment gardens to find their kitchens empty and dark.

When we finished, we had a village of cottage stones sitting on the lawn, a kindergarten celebration of all that was timeless and quintessential about the village itself and the people who lived in it.

The big ones went home to become doorstops and paperweights. The little ones went off to the Women's Institute, where they fetched 50 pence each at the next jumble sale.

Chagall himself would have been proud, I think. 🐗

DREAMS OF ELEPHANTS
Thomas Palakeel

For a middle-class boy growing up in the 1960s, in a Roman Catholic pocket of the southern Indian state of Kerala, the most acceptable ambition was to become a missionary. ✎ My mother was probably thinking that I might even become a bishop. ✎ Once, as I was pretending to be asleep, I overheard her whisper to my sisters that I was the most innocent of her boys, that my face itself was the manifestation of innocence, that I really had the Great Call, the Vocation. ✎

But I had decided to become an elephant hunter. The autobiography of a walrus-mustached elephant hunter named Ittan Mathewkutty, being serialized in the Sunday paper, had such an impact on me that I started dreaming about dropping out of school and going away with a mahout. When my cousin ran away from home, I envied him and shocked everyone at home by describing him as a brave boy.

Once I followed a domestic elephant a few miles and finally worked up enough courage to talk to the mahout about my interest in becoming an elephant hunter like Ittan Mathewkutty. The sinister-looking mahout smiled as he chewed betel nuts, exhibiting all his teeth dripping with red betel juice, but he did not say a word. Except for his periodic commands to the huge animal walking ahead of us with about a ton of palm leaves tucked in between its tusks (its dinner), the whole atmosphere was quiet.

About an hour later, we reached a river that was drying up very early in the summer. The mahout asked the elephant to step into the water. The animal turned around and looked at me with its tiny eyes, laid down the palm leaves, and obediently entered the pool. The water level rose and soaked my feet. I backed up. The mahout also stepped into the water. With a coconut husk, he started scrubbing the endless black mass submerged in the greenish water. I observed him studiously, admiring his hard work; soon he started wiping sweat off his forehead. When my legs ached, I perched on the low branch of a jackfruit tree and watched the mahout make the elephant turn sides and scrub the other side.

After the elephant was bathed, the mahout himself took a dip in an upper corner of the pool. When the majestic black elephant, with pink spots on its massive earlobes and humungous trunk, and the long, well-rounded, swordlike tusks shining after the wash, emerged from the pool, I applauded in great joy. I knew that I would certainly dedicate my life for one such indescribable beauty.

This time the mahout looked up to the tree I was perched on and smiled: "What do you think?"

"My dear tusker," I said.

"This one belongs to the gods." The mahout meant that the elephant was the property of a Hindu temple.

"I want to become a mahout," I said.

"Didn't you want to become an elephant hunter awhile ago?" The man laughed.

"That's when I grow up," I said.

"These boys!" he said. "Go home and study."

"Could you give me an elephant hair?" I asked.

Now the mahout was buckling up the huge metal chain elephants wear around their backs. I loved the deep clanging of these chains, and I heard this sound often in my dreams.

"An elephant hair to make a ring for my mother," I added.

The mahout smiled again, unsheathed his fierce-looking knife with his right hand, grabbed the elephant's moving tail with his left, and cut out a long hair from the end of the tail. He handed it to me with a smile. "Go home and do your homework."

As I stood there gazing at the miraculous, strong, wirelike elephant hair resting on my palms, the mahout walked ahead, uttering those mysterious commands which the noble animal obeyed like a child. And I ran home with the elephant's hair.

The elephant's hair had provoked serious discussions in our family about my divine future. My sisters confirmed that I wouldn't settle for anything less than the immortality of the walrus-mustached elephant hunter. And I was banned from reading the autobiography of Ittan Mathewkutty and the Mandrake the Magician cartoons.

The censorship was painful, especially because I was feeling deprived of heroes to identify with and to mold a fanciful world around. The previous several years' heroes, Neil Armstrong, Edwin Aldrin, and Michael Collins, were not in the newspapers anymore. Man's historic landing on the moon had become just another date in history. However, I could always go back to my Apollo II album that I had created with black and white pictures cut out of newspapers and magazines.

My favorite ones were the three family photos: I admired the Armstrong-Aldrin-Collins boys and girls, revered the wives, and deified the great astronaut trio in those pictures. The picture of Edwin Aldrin descending the ladder of the lunar module never failed to intrigue me. There was another newspaper picture of the trio in Bombay a few months after the landing on the moon, and this particular picture made me impatient about my boyhood. I wished to grow up fast.

The tension about me at home was aggravated one night when I did not return from my father's village store, where I was sent to pick up groceries. On my way back, I met a gang of Hindu boys who were going to a temple festival. Even though Christian boys were not welcomed to enter the Hindu temple, my good friends invited me to join them. Though I was taught in catechism classes horrible things about the myriads of Hindu gods, I decided to follow my friends to the festival.

When I returned after midnight, my father asked my mother not to feed me: The punishment was first of all for going to the Hindu temple, and then for returning home late.

Ashamed by the punishment, I went to bed, but my mind was filled with the vivid scenes of the festival: decorated elephants bearing Hindu icons wrapped in red silk, a dozen drummers orchestrating the loudest ritual tunes, conch blowers, the Brahman priests, two old men fanning the deity atop the elephant with a pair of exquisite fans made of feathers, women dressed in golden-brocaded saris leading the procession with oil lamps, and thousands watching their lord pass by with attentive devotion.

In the morning, I declared my fasting protest to the whole family and hid myself in the attic. I was seriously planning to starve myself to death. I had read in my textbook how Gandhi did this and brought the British to their knees. When I didn't go down to the kitchen, turning down both breakfast and lunch, my mother came to the attic door late in the afternoon and said that she accepted defeat.

I clambered down the ladder without speaking a word. My sisters were all watching this from different vantage points. Lunch was ready for me on the table.

"This child hasn't eaten anything for the last 24 hours," my mother said as she served more curries on my plate. After I had eaten a few rice balls dipped in the curry, my mother asked my sister Molly to bring a banana for me as a dessert.

Molly went up the ladder and screamed, staring into the attic where only a bare banana stalk was hanging from the roof beam: "Mom, he ate all the bananas!"

Everyone in the household laughed and rushed to the dining room to see the new Gandhi. My mother laughed, too. I didn't. When my father came home from the store that night, my mother told him about my fasting and about the two dozen bananas that had disappeared from the attic. My father also laughed, but he said that if I was let out freely into the village anymore, I might end up like a filthy mahout: low class, crude, immoral, eventually poor.

When everyone talked about my mahout-heroes in such abysmally low terms, it made me wonder what could be more adventurous than becoming the absolute master of an elephant.

In the tempestuous monsoon at the end of that summer, our century-old school building collapsed. In the new school year, about two-thirds of the students were to be accommodated in the Catholic parish hall and the rest in the small auditorium at the Hindu temple.

I learned that my parents were planning to send me to an English school. I hoped to avoid going to the school by winning my mother's confidence. I would bribe her with a secret gift: a ring made of fine gold, threaded around the elephant's hair. But my parents wanted to save me from class degradation and elephant worship that threatened my future. Soon I left the safety of Thidanad and my Malayalam world and was sent to the English school. 🐘

MUSIC IN THE AIR: IMMIGRANTS LEARN ENGLISH IN A POST OFFICE

Cynthia Dresser

The back road to Salinas from the Monterey Peninsula provides a change from the buffeting sea breezes, taking you away from the dunes and cresting just above the Salinas River. 🐀

After the bridge the road narrows, carries you swiftly down toward the inviting scene below, past newly plowed fields, their rows even and steady as a drumbeat, past the lettuce: row upon row of green leaf, interspersed with rows and rows of purple leaf, then on past blue-green leaves wrapped around white cauliflower. Fields stretch as far as the eye can see in the morning light across the Salinas Valley.

Salinas town is there, ringed by hills and protected by fields, fields tended by hatted workers in colorful clothes, their neckerchiefs pulled up over their noses. Most are Mexicans.

They come to work in the fields. They have names like Eudoxio and Féliz and Guadalupe, Eriberto and Socorro and Mariceli, Altagracia and Heraclio. Many have family already in the area. Spanish is the language and music in the air, lending a definite other-world feeling to Salinas, a town with an estimated Mexican population of more than 40,000 out of 100,000.

Some of the issues facing the Mexican population include housing, wages, and field conditions, but the major issue is language. For while the Spanish-speaking community is large, English is still the majority language and many ordinary transactions must be done in English. Fortunately, Salinas has a well-established adult education system, involving 20,000 students. About 4,000 are taking English as a second language (ESL), with Hispanics, particularly Mexicans, as the majority. About 2,000 study English in classrooms off the main lobby in the local post office.

Like the post office in any self-respecting town, the Old Post Office in downtown Salinas is a hub of activity. The morning sun, shining in through the long paned windows, its light filtering through perennially dusty venetian

165

blinds, warms the lobby and highlights the tiny brass and glass mail compartments numbered in red and gold. As people briskly arrive for the day's mail, the air is filled with the sound of footsteps across the old brick floor, the snaps and clicks of many mail compartments being opened and hurriedly shut, and snatches of conversations.

A line forms within the maroon plastic ropes, people waiting for Vern or Vivian or Lenny at their counter sections. Overheard pieces of conversation might be in Spanish, in Vietnamese, English, black English, or post office English:

"Book 'a 25's."

"There y'are."

Around the edges of the lobby are the students dressed in their best, expectant, ready. Before class and at break they lounge against the windowsills or at the extra counters, off to one side, but visible, speaking to each other, watching the activity.

From down the hall come sounds of the pronunciation class: "seat-sit; beat-bit." A teacher passes through, pausing to talk with students in Spanish. Doors in the lobby are constantly opening and closing; there is movement, there is a sense of aliveness.

Many of the people attracted to this area are rural folk and have had little formal schooling in Mexico. Many begin their formal education in an adult school, bringing with them pockets of fluency or knowledge of English from their various and broad experiences.

But before they can acquire literacy in their second language, it would be helpful, even necessary, for them to work toward literacy in their first language. The task is neither small nor insignificant, but they are used to working; many have worked at manual labor since an early age.

Maricela has worked in the fields since the second grade, and still does, while raising three children and attending English class. Féliz was a corn and beans farmer in Mexico; here he goes to school in the morning and works as a field hand in the afternoon. Because there's a waiting list for classes in his town, Heraclio drives 50 miles to the night class after a day of working.

"Hi, Luis!"

"Hello, Manuel! How are you?"

The morning begins in a bustle of greetings. Rumaldo arranges the desks in a semicircle and Eulalia and the others help. Maria gives the flowers fresh water, Ernesto cleans the blackboard, and I unload the day's books and papers, amid a lot of conversation, touching base from the day before.

While English is the language of the classroom, the goal is communication, so pieces of Spanish and sometimes Chinese float on the air as we get settled.

"Maybe I working *mañana*."

"*Cho-san*," I greet Pai in his language.

"Good morning," he answers in English.

Today Ernesto is in charge of the attendance sheet and he fills it out, writing in the date, the hours, my name. It is passed around for each student to sign.

"You're too late," he tells Benjamin, who is just coming in. Benjamin sits down in a flood of greetings. Ernesto gives him the sheet to sign.

"It's never too late," I reply.

"How are you? Who are you?" We play the careful listening game to sharpen their agility out on the street, to tell the small difference, and to learn to respond to what they actually hear, not what they expect to hear.

"Remember, 'I don't know' is a good answer," I remind them. We review "Huh? What? I don't understand. Please repeat," as ways to keep a conversation open; I act out the concept by demonstrating.

"Ask me a question," I tell one of the more experienced students.

"What's the date?" he responds.

I drop my eyes. "Conversation closed," I say, my eyes still averted. Suddenly my arms fly open, I look directly at each student, and say in a strong voice, "I don't understand!" Then I add, "Conversation—open."

Other days I toss an imaginary ball to each person as I ask a question, and they toss it back as they give the answer. "A conversation is a job for two people," I say. They know "job." I keep the language uncomplicated and manageable, building on what is known. What is known is surprising, and in order for it to show up, students get plenty of opportunity to respond creatively.

Long before anyone is expected to produce complex sentences, we are practicing ways to express ideas and feelings. We work with emotions and body language through role play and mime. Using a page of mime photographs from their dictionary, they imitate the faces, making their classmates guess which photo they are imitating, thus eliminating the necessity of pronouncing some more difficult words, like "ecstasy."

We make "mood cubes" out of folded index cards. They choose six

167

different moods from the photos, copying the words from the book. Eudoxio, who at 54 is beginning his formal education, always keeps his cube showing "determined," which really fits him. Each morning we put the mood cubes on our desks and check each other. "Fine" doesn't suffice between friends. During the morning, as moods change, the cubes change and "Hungry" appears, or "Proud."

I use students to model for each other, to reduce the stress of trying to achieve native-like pronunciation, since communication is our goal. Once when we were practicing the sound of the "th," only shy, soft-spoken Hijinio could do it. The other students said it was because he played the trumpet. This brought on a quick poll to see who played music. The next day we had an impromptu music session at break time.

This cooperative atmosphere builds trust and confidence, both within each student and within the group, which includes me. I act as facilitator, sometime-instigator, observer, and always, encourager. I never think in terms of what they don't know or can't do. We work with what we have, and emphasize what they do know, applying it to survival English skills.

Self-esteem, self-awareness, and confidence are major issues in this group of pre-beginners with little or no previous formal education. We begin with the alphabet, putting ourselves in alphabetical order, like a long snake. Later we do body order: Everyone has a card with a body part and we have to arrange ourselves from head to toe. English is spoken, but nobody is worrying. There is a lot of laughing every day as we carry out our tasks: to feel good and promote learning and acquisition doing it!

In the early stages they also learn to say what they do in their country, where their self-esteem is based. This can help them project a more vivid image of themselves here, even while experiencing language and culture shock. They learn ways to preserve their natural dignity in a society that may ask too many questions at times:

"Rumaldo, where were you last night?"

"I'd rather not say."

"Do you have a bank account?"

"I'm sorry—that's my business."

One day on an impulse, I handed my pointer to a student who was speaking softly and ineffectively. It is really difficult to mutter, "I'm from Jalisco, Mexico," with a stick in your hand. His voice immediately took a strong and authoritative tone. He handed the stick to Hijinio and the same thing happened. Now whenever anyone speaks ineffectively, other students say, "Give him the stick." Luis still puts his hand on his chest and bellows, "I'm from Mexico!" And no one ever gives him the teacher's stick.

English class at the Post Office, in the words of an advanced student, is "Hectic because of hall traffic, and interesting because of so much activity. But there's not enough privacy."

The high visibility of English class at the Post Office seems important and somewhat symbolic: Voluntarily learning a second language is about letting down cultural barriers, widening the possibilities for new jobs, new friends, new confidence.

This being done in full view of the public emphasizes that it is a public occasion—it is not just the private concern of a few individuals trying to improve their lives or meet the conditions of a new country. ❧

Learning Where To Start
Ted Berkman

Cairo, where I was stationed in the 1940s as a government intelligence analyst and later as a radio correspondent, lingers in my mind as a kaleidoscope of memories: the Giza pyramids, dim and majestic from my balcony; mosques and minarets lighting up the Old Quarter after dark in a dazzling Arabian Nights display; goats wandering placidly along the banks of biblical canals. ☜ Scents and sounds float back: the mingled spices of a canvas-roofed bazaar blended into the heavy sweetness of night jasmine along the Nile; the lonely piercing wail of a muezzin and the murmur of Mayfair accents on the terrace of Shepheard's Hotel, where British colonels gathered to sip their imperial lemonade. ☜

Over the years, some images of Cairo have remained indelible. Others have changed, like the shifting patterns of a shuffled kaleidoscope, in response to random stimulation. Awakened by the squawk of auto horns in New York, I have heard again the din of traffic along Suleiman Pasha Street, the braying of donkeys, the early morning slap of dusty carpets against balcony railings. When political storms broke over Egypt in the early 1950s, I was carried back to the stinging contrasts of the colonial era: posh Western country clubs amid the hovels of rural *fellaheen*; the well-groomed Egyptian senator who, gazing down from his Medici-style mansion at ragged Cairenes swarming over an ancient trolley, likened his countrymen to "so many flies."

Two decades after Egypt I was back again under blue subtropical skies, this time writing films in Hollywood. Restless in what I found an oppressively competitive milieu, I had begun an inward search for more enduring values. This gained impetus with the arrival of the space age, bearing its unmistakable message of human interdependence. Groping toward a future in a more sharing, caring universe, I discovered that I was looking back on a newly illumined past. From the great anonymous mass of Egypt, as crowded with figures as an Orozco mural, faces all but forgotten leaped into sudden consciousness. I remembered Ibrahim, a "houseboy" of 40, struggling stubbornly through lessons in reading from his 12-year-old son. And Said Yassin, who to promote the dignity of workers in his small glass factory created unheard-of facilities for study and recreation. And I remembered Mustafa.

I first encountered him, a fellow boarder in Mme. Dufond's pension, at breakfast: a quiet, wiry little man half-hidden behind a luxuriant gray mustache. Despite the heat of the Cairo summer—it would be well over 100 degrees by noon—he wore a brown tie with his immaculate white shirt.

"Good morning, sir." Sharp humorous black eyes looked up from the hard-boiled egg on his plate. "I trust you have slept well?" His manner was polite but not deferential. We introduced ourselves. He took a last swallow of thick Turkish coffee, picked up a small leather briefcase, plopped a red fez on his head, and was gone.

A few days later we met again at teatime, when Cairo yawns its way back to life after the long midday siesta. Mustafa was in Madame's parlor, sipping hot mint tea and sifting through a pile of newspapers: two Arabic dailies, the English-language *Egyptian Gazette* and *La Bourse Egyptienne*. From his laborious scanning of the *Bourse* headlines, it was obvious that his French was limited; I sensed a hunger for a wider world.

That evening, Mme. Dufond provided a little fill-in. Mustafa was a civil servant, some sort of irrigation engineer, who every morning made his rounds through the nearby villages of the Nile countryside. He was a widower with a son apprenticed to an archaeologist at Luxor. And he was "pour un Egyptien, très cultivé."

The following week, I was alone in the parlor preparing for a late-night broadcast when Mustafa came in. On impulse, I asked if he knew anything about the early history of Cairo's Coptic community. He nodded, disappeared into his room, and returned with a year-old clipping from the *Egyptian Gazette*. It had exactly the material I wanted.

Thereafter, when I needed quick, accurate information I knew where to go. Mustafa in turn was happy to dip into my small English-language library,

171

devouring poetry and politics alike but rarely venturing any comment.

Came September and a rising, suffocating Nile. To my mild astonishment, Mustafa did not curtail his schedule. On the contrary, his workday seemed longer. And the bureaucratic briefcase was now supplemented by a bulging knapsack. I suppressed my curiosity—for a while. Finally I asked about the knapsack.

Mustafa smiled, a little sadly, and lifted its flap. A can of New Zealand beef came into view, and a bar of chocolate. "Most of the *fellaheen* in my district are barely at subsistence level," he said. "They broil in the summer sun, shiver at night in winter. What good does it do for me simply to give them clever advice, then leave them to shift for themselves? A man who is hungry is not going to put his mind on anything else. So I bring a bit of beef, powdered milk for the children, a blanket. With the necessities taken care of he may be encouraged to learn, to become all he is capable of becoming. Who knows what treasures may lie like seeds in his brain, waiting only for the proper nourishment? After all, we irrigate the fields. . . ."

I stared at the knapsack, aware of Cairo's minuscule salaries and of the city's war-inflated prices. "Isn't that very costly for you?"

Again the sad smile, "It's an investment in humanity. Do you know anything more worth supporting?" 🐖

'I'D LIKE TO MAKE YOU A CHAIR'
Pippa Stuart

It is terrifying to wake toward midnight, emerging from uneasy dreams and sensing that someone is there, stirring outside in the shadows. ❧ This winter night, the first thing we heard was a faint creaking, then the sound of a door being pushed stealthily open. ❧

All at once there came a loud crash of something being knocked over and the thump of someone falling heavily. We approached cautiously, remembering warnings to avoid confrontation at all costs, never approaching a burglar who may be armed or violent.

At the kitchen door lay an upturned chair with a broken leg, and beside it sprawled the intruder, our first housebreaker. The telephone was close at hand, to dial the police in a matter of minutes. We had to act quickly before he did. Slumped there, he was the most unlikely of thieves, lumbering, clumsily built, with spiky ginger hair and a gaunt, grizzled face. He looked a born bungler, as if anything he took up would be botched, burglary included. He was staring from us to the telephone, making no attempt to rise to his feet.

"Don't 'phone them," he said at last in a husky whisper. "It was finding the door unlocked that did it. There's something about a locked door . . . I'd rather be deid than be sent back. I promise I'll go straight." He was shivering, his face almost greenish in tinge with terror. He was far more afraid of us than we were of him. "What were you up to?" we asked, still hesitating to pick up the receiver.

He stammered out an explanation of sorts and a picture arose of someone weak rather than wicked. He was newly released and finding work was difficult for ex-prisoners. In all he blurted out we heard echoes of a key turning, a door clanging, felt the intolerable desolation and frailty of the

173

human heart, all the horror of captivity, however much deserved. Which was the greater crime, a bungled housebreaking or the handing over of so wretched a soul to the police?

There are sudden impulses in life, either to be rejected as mere folly, momentary madness, or else instantly obeyed, times when you step into the unknown, trust the untrustworthy. All right, we told him. "You've promised to go straight. We believe you."

Our intruder stumbled to his feet and picked up the broken chair. He tried to say something, his jaw moved, nothing came out. "I learned a bit of joinery in there," he brought out at last in his gruff whisper. "I'll come back one day and mend your chair."

We hoped he wouldn't. He had scared us stiff and wrung our hearts. He went off down the garden, a hulking figure in a tattered, greasy jacket, starting violently when an owl hooted. He stood for a moment in a patch of dappled moonlight, looking up at the trees that grew all around our home, then disappeared along the deep woodland lane, among elms, limes, and birches.

For a long time we couldn't get the sight of that stricken face from our minds, nor the sound of that desperate, pleading voice. "I have been one acquainted with the night," Robert Frost wrote. Our would-be burglar was such a one. The broken kitchen chair was so vivid a reminder of that midnight visitation that we stacked it out of sight in a garden hut.

We had almost forgotten the episode when, one morning in early spring, we started as we opened the back door. There he stood, our bungling burglar, instantly recognizable, only a little less haggard and a good deal tidier. "I've not forgotten," he said. "I've a week's holiday from work and so I'm back to mend yon chair."

He was so deeply serious that we led him to the shed where, along with the chair, wood from a dismantled wardrobe and dressing table was piled high against the wall. He eyed it all, touched a panel of walnut, ran his hand slowly down some oak. For such a lumpish, blundering, awkwardly constructed man he had surprisingly fine hands. "I like the feel of wood," he said.

By the end of the morning he had mended the chair. He held it out to us awkwardly, gulping. He still had something to communicate and communication was not his strong point. We waited. "All that wood lying out there doing nowt," he began. "I'd like fine to make you a chair, not a kitchen one, a *real* one."

"A real chair!" we said dubiously, but he was wandering away on his own

174

train of thought. "When I was in yon prison workshop, I kept thinking about chairs, something you sit in to talk to friends. I've never done much of that, squandered away my life, you'd say. . . ." His voice trailed away. "Go ahead and make us a chair," we said.

The next day he turned up with a bag of tools, a hone, a plane, sandpaper, a bottle of linseed oil, and shellac. We were going to greet him, then realized we didn't know his name. "Call me Chairlie," he said. He measured the wood, stroked it. "The chair's still in my heid," he said. "It'll take shape as I work at it."

The main fact in life became the creation of Charlie's chair. At first we had joked about it, asking when it would be ready, but he was so profoundly serious that we were ashamed. You couldn't be facetious with Charlie. When we passed the shed, we had glimpses of his face and it wore a quite new expression, a kind of rapture, and we would look away as if intruding on something intensely private. "Blessed is he who has found his work. Let him ask no other blessedness."

Charlie was very definite about one thing. "You're no' to see it till it's ready, mind! Gie's your word that you'll no' come and keek at it." What was going on in his head, we wondered, as he honed and carved, planed and polished? Was the act of creation exorcising that dark time? When he left at night, he lingered with us for a moment, giving off a distinctive odor of linseed oil. "Aye, aye, it's coming on," was all he would say, then he would be off.

One morning in mid-May we heard him call to us with a funny, excited note in his gruff voice. "It's ready!" He opened the door of the shed like an artist unveiling his painting for the appraisal of the curious and the critical. For days he had lived alone with his wood, and now he had to offer the result of his toil to our judgment. As he had once looked between us and a phone, now he looked from us to the chair, eagerly, hopefully.

What had we really expected? Another botched job? It was one thing to repair a broken chair leg, quite another to construct a new chair. We could only stare, nearer to tears than to words. Charlie's great hands, infinitely sensitive, had sandpapered and oiled and smoothed till the wood was like satin. "I've had a tussle and a trauchle with yon wood," he said with pride.

We would never see the like of this chair again. It stood for something beyond itself, for an act of liberation. It was not a Van Gogh-like chair, not yet a Chippendale or Sheraton, but it had a fine, clean line, its own elegance. It was the kind of chair you could sit in at ease with yourself and the world.

175

"It's beautiful," we said. "You must sell it for a lot of money and set up a carpentry shop of your own."

"That chair will never be for sale!" he exclaimed almost angrily. "It's yours. I'll never make another that means so much. When you sit in it, you'll mind how I gied you my word and kept it." He swept up the shavings and gathered together his tools. "I'll be on my way," he said.

Spring comes late in Scotland, but while Charlie had been working, the garden and the woods had grown daily greener and the trees were now at their loveliest. He was better with wood than with words, but now, as he looked up at the elms and birches for the last time, he became almost poetic. "There's the providers," he said, touching the bark of a silver birch.

As we watched him go, we were tantalized by the "what ifs" that life poses. What if he hadn't gone straight, what if we had regretted our impulse? And yet if we hadn't followed our instinct, there would be no chair and maybe no Charlie. After all, we thought, no one has ever reproached the good Samaritan for his impulsive behavior. ✍

An American On Kosygin Street
Jeremy Bransten

Morning sun lights up our room at Eaglet Youth Complex, a 15-story hotel exclusively for young people and situated in suburban Moscow. 🪳 I lie in bed watching a cockroach forage on my night table. 🪳 Hesitantly, it enters a "Roach Motel," brought by my roommate from New York. 🪳 He cheers. 🪳 "Works better than at home," he announces. 🪳

Beyond the window sprawls the city, surprisingly huge, gray, and dusty-looking, with row upon row of prefab apartment blocks, their concrete facings badly weathered. Many factories belch smoke into the sky. Moscow appears raw and recently built, its urban landscape punctuated by overgrown greenery and garish propaganda signs. A crimson banner above Kosygin Street, which fronts our complex, announces: "GLASNOST WIDENS THE SCOPE OF DEMOCRACY FOR THE 70TH ANNIVERSARY OF THE REVOLUTION."

In the elevator en route to breakfast, I fall into conversation with several Ukrainian high-school students on vacation from Kiev. One of them, Sasha, sidles up to me. "Will you let us see your weapons?" he asks.

"Weapons?"

"Come on, we're not so naive. We know what goes on in America. Did you bring your guns?"

I reply that "Roach Motels" do the job in Moscow.

We walk around the lobby and converse on a variety of topics, or rather we talk at one another. Americans and Ukrainians firmly hold to their initial convictions. We part amicably, but I'm disturbed. I have come to the Soviet Union with nine teammates. We range in age from 15 to 18, high school sophomores, juniors, and seniors. We're here to compete in a 50-nation Russian language and literature contest held only once every three years;

Russian language and literature contest held only once every three years: the Olympiada This is the sixth such event, and our group, winners in a runoff series across the United States, is sponsored and paid for by the Association of American Teachers of Russian.

Surely, I tell myself, the real goal to our being here is to foster understanding. Now, I wonder if that's possible. Russian we share as the common language with everyone we encounter; but words in different cultures take on different, even opposite, meanings.

My roommates and I find that on this noncompetition day we're free to go where we wish, unescorted. We decide to explore the city center, especially Red Square. Maybe at her center of gravity we'll hear, and understand, "Mother Russia's" heartbeat.

Outside the complex, we're accosted by two tough-looking 20-year-olds in Levis, Reeboks, and muscle shirts.

"You Americans?" asks the taller one in English. He introduces himself as Dimitri. Before we can answer, his companion eyes my feet and says they wish to speak to us of friendship. We stroll toward the subway station at Lenin Prospect, and talk turns to my New Balance sneakers.

"What you want for shoes?" asks Dimitri, who sticks to English. "How you say, to improve myself, yes? I got flags, lacquer boxes, football jerseys—I used to be on Dynamo soccer team [unlikely, this being the most prestigious of Soviet sports teams]—military hats. . . ." To emphasize the last, he opens a plastic bag and reveals a blue and gold Navy officer's hat. I catch the whiff of a cologne Russian men love to douse on themselves: "Red Moscow for Men."

Inside the station, the woman in charge of watching the escalators slumps in her booth, peaked red cap covering her eyes: the face of "100 percent employment," as propaganda proclaims? The subway itself runs very smoothly. A noiseless blue train whisks us the 10 or so miles to the Kremlin in 15 minutes.

Red Square is full of soldiers and large signs, like "HERE WE DON'T SMOKE!" We manage, finally, to shed our Russians, my sneakers still on my feet, and decide to try one of the large hotels for lunch, surely better fare than at Eaglet. The Intourist hotel lobby is filled with globe-trotters in Hawaiian shirts and shorts. They chat loudly, in English, about their touristic forays. A few yuppie types in jackets and bow ties sit on comfortable maroon couches. Upstairs, at the restaurant, the hostess shakes her head at the

178

three of us while yelling into the telephone: "Tell the Germans not before 3:30."

At the Hotel Moscow we can't eat because it's "sanitary hour." Nevertheless, a Supreme Soviet delegate brushes past us to a table. In the beautifully set dining room of the National Hotel, the waiters are busy serving themselves. They expect a group next day, we are told, so cannot possibly serve us. Up against a true Iron Curtain that crashes down whenever service is involved in a land without incentives, we haggle with a reluctant cabdriver for the trip back to Kosygin Street. There, we face greasy meat bits afloat in broth. We smile at the Mongolian team sitting nearby. They avoid our eyes.

In contrast, as I finish dessert, excellent ice cream (Soviet ice cream, vanilla, is good and seems readily available), I am engaged in conversation by a Chinese girl who eagerly exchanges addresses. I ask what she thinks of Moscow. She says she finds it very green. She wants to know if I wear braces on my teeth for fashion's sake.

As the northern sun disappears in a pale, drawn-out twilight, I find myself unexpectedly at Zagorsk, a country village 50 miles north of Moscow. Here the most beautiful and important Russian monastery still functions. On its grounds, beneath blue and gold onion domes, peasant women collect holy water from an outdoor fountain. Orthodox monks in flowing black capes sweep along the walkways, occasionally stopping to offer advice to devout parishioners. We're with our regular guide, assigned to us for our twelve-day stay. She looks at the monks with suspicion and chidingly asks: "Are they really so innocent?" That leads me to think about a question on our competition briefing sheet: "What does the Soviet Union mean for you?"

In the contest itself, for which I've been preparing through my first three high school years and with a stint at Harvard summer school, I mention cultural achievements, territorial vastness, and the need for mutual comprehension for mutual survival. But my last day in Moscow I get a more personal answer while exploring near Yaroslavl train station, gateway to Siberia and Central Asia.

I watch an old Uzbek try crossing the wide avenue leading to the station. With his walking stick, white turban, flowing beard, and indigo robe he is out of "The Thousand and One Nights." After several attempts, and ignoring the underground pedestrian passage marked "To Station," he finally hobbles across—and immediately is swallowed by the milling crowd of the terminus. Try as I will, I can't spot him again.

Was he a vision, some sort of illusion? Is the Soviet Union so diverse and contradictory that its union is illusory? At home, I begin to wonder if my whole trip wasn't a dream.

No, a few kopecks rustle in my pocket, a gold medal and diploma lie on my bed, and also the offer of a five-year scholarship to Moscow University. My gaze lingers on a miniature icon of Semiofan, a miracle worker and former monk at Zagorsk. Our guide—so hostile while showing us the monastery— gave it to me as a farewell gift. How Russian in its generosity, and in the implied paradox. How long an undertaking to answer what the Soviet Union truly means to me. ☙

Jogging In Japan
Elizabeth Brown

It's another scorching day in Kyoto—so hot I don't need an alarm clock. 🐚 By 6 a.m. the sun is streaming through the *shoji*—sliding doors of opaque glass—filling my small room with sunshine, spilling onto my bed on the floor. 🐚 Quickly I dress for my morning jog along the river. 🐚

As an American living and working in this fast-paced country, I value this time to be alone with my thoughts and the peaceful surroundings. Keeps my soul toned, and my body trim for modeling assignments.

Since it hasn't rained for days, the river is calm. The air is clean and only early-morning humid. It smells of little fish and tall trees. Rhythmically the gravel scrunches beneath my feet. All is quiet except for the few cars and Japanese-sized trucks on their way to work.

I jog past a couple of elderly gentlemen—one in a white sweat suit, being towed briskly by his dog, another in a traditional robe of dark brown linen, moving slowly, bent over his knobby walking stick. After the second bridge I pass the old man who does *tai chi*—Chinese exercise, a sort of slow kung fu—every morning on the riverbank. His slow, controlled movements remind me of early mornings in China—my home before Japan—where old people rise at dawn to stretch their limbs and soothe their minds before the day's work begins. I feel a kinship with folks who share the secrets of morning serenity.

A few fishermen dot the riverbank; the rhythm of the gravel is broken as I leap over scattered bamboo fishing poles and rusty pails. The sun is hot on my back as I continue along the river's path. Only the *tsuru*—white cranes —have commenced communal activity, but quietly. They soar. They wade. They dive for fish. Even the pigeons are listless in this heat, except when they waddle aside to let me pass.

181

At the northern tip of my loop I am in the country, surrounded by rice and vegetable fields. On spring and fall mornings, when I run later, I see groups of schoolchildren—in uniforms, caps, and knapsacks—playing on their way to school. They stare and giggle awkwardly when I run by; if I speak to them they laugh and run for cover. But this morning it's too early to see them.

Now I come to my favorite spot: the horse barn. I jog across the road, into the barn, and greet the horses—in Japanese. Would they understand English? I inhale deeply, eyes closed; for a moment I am back home in my father's horse barn. Summer is my favorite time on the farm in Michigan, but I haven't been there for two years.

Second half of the loop, sun in my face.

"*Ohayo gozaimasu*," pants a familiar voice. She smiles—we're friends without names—and nods her visor. Maybe she's a housewife—as most women are—who returns home to prepare her husband for work and her children for school. Yet she is an unusual sight—a middle-aged woman jogging alone every morning, rain or shine (and at a faster clip than I!). I wonder why she jogs so diligently. Is it to keep fit?

A thin breeze rustles the grass along the path. The old women who tend the riverbank are ready to start working. Chattering, they assemble, carrying trowels, rakes, and towels. They're dressed in traditional blue cotton pants and little jackets, with white hand towels resting on the tops of their heads. A funny sight, I think. But perhaps they find my wide-soled shoes, sweat-soaked tank top, and punky sunglasses just as silly. Whatever, we always exchange greetings—bows and smiles—as I jog by.

It's hot, and my 10 kilometers are finished. Stopping by a place with easy access to the river, I look around to make sure no one is watching, take off my shoes and socks, and wade to my knees in the icy river. Ah, heaven.

On the way back to my room, I stop by the neighbor's abundant flower bed for a whiff of some new blossoms. The flowers come and go so quickly in the summer. The earth feels cold under my feet, but I must be careful that no one sees my delight; the Japanese do *not* approve of bare feet outdoors.

By now my room smells of tatami—the straw matting used for floors in traditional Japanese homes. The smell reminds me of summer haymows back home. But here we live, work, and sleep on the plant. I'm glad the mats in my room are still fresh.

I turn on the floor fan and begin my morning chores: fold the sheets,

182

hang the *futon*, or cotton mattress, on the railing outside my window, vacuum the floor, dust the table in my room, and turn on the TV for my morning French lesson in Japanese.

I wander outside and bring in laundry from my little clothesline. Already my landlady is in the garden pulling weeds from around the rocks. I think that's her serenity before the day. When she sees me watching, she smiles, stands to straighten her apron, and giggles with her hand covering her mouth. "*Ohayo gozaimasu, Riza-san*," she says with a bowing nod.

"*Ohayo gozaimasu, Ueda-san*," I return, with a quick bow. We talk about the weather and the garden—all in Japanese. How I wish I could talk about more personal things—ask her what it's like to be a single woman raising teen-age sons in modern Japan, or what she thinks about when she's pulling weeds. Sometimes when I see her watching TV by herself or sitting alone at the kitchen table, she seems lonely. This morning she looks happy.

Towel and toiletries container in hand, I walk across the garden to her house, where I use the *ofuro*—Japanese bath. I stop to look at the *koi*—big carp, once I heard one speak—when splash! the frog jumps in. Happens every morning. 🪭

THE COMMODORE WAS HOME
John Yemma

Others, who'd been stationed there in the halcyon 1950s, told me they used to enjoy the St. George. ✆ They talked of breezes wafting in off the Mediterranean, sun-lapped verandas, lovely old souks, and the showy, Las Vegas-style nightlife just minutes away. ✆

That seemed wonderful to me. But it was legend by the time I got there.

The St. George was destroyed. My home was the Commodore. It was up the hill from the St. George; much dowdier; secreted among the low-rise buildings of Beirut's crowded Hamra Street. It was less of a prize, less strategic a location for the armies, gangs, and freebooters who roamed west Beirut when I was there in the early '80s.

But the Commodore was home—a somewhat quiet place to sleep and get an OK meal. It wasn't a hotel you checked into and out of antiseptically, as you might in London, New York, or San Francisco. You *had to* know the staff, the regulars, the oddities. You knew that somehow, when everything else fell apart, Fuad Salah kept the Commodore running.

My first night at the Commodore, during a relatively quiet summer, a colleague was worried he might be kidnapped. He slept in the closet of his room. That seemed funny at the time.

Two years later, having been in and out of the Commodore many times, I heard sonic booms and watched leaflets float down outside my window. These announced that the city was going to be stormed by the Israeli Army the next day. I spent a sleepless night listening to the artillery booming south of the city and considering just when I might roll off the bed and crawl into the closet.

There were many, many times like that. But not every day was the eve of the end of the world. There were lulls, time for jaunts through the gorgeous hills surrounding Beirut, trips to see a dance troupe or window-shopping in the Hamra Street boutiques. There were even mornings of jogging on the Corniche, the seafront road.

Always, it was back home to the Commodore, where Fuad kept things orderly, food available, telexes humming.

The family table was the horseshoe-shaped bar in the lobby of the hotel. Around it, all manner of correspondent, spy, ne'er-do-well, and information-peddler appeared and disappeared. One could schmooze with other hacks, sidle up to a key figure in the PLO, or organize a trip to some of the forlorn French restaurants flickering like dying campfires in the wasted city.

It was at the Commodore that I met Abed. He was one of the taxi drivers so necessary to deal with in order to reconnoiter the streets, camps, and faraway regions of that beautiful, ruined nation.

Abed was cool and kind; he didn't get excited at a checkpoint or under fire. He was like an old uncle, my ambassador to the strange world of Lebanon, driving his big Pontiac through the crowded streets.

One Saturday, during one of the inexplicable lulls in the madness, Abed agreed to drive my wife and me out of Beirut, across the mountains, and into the Bekaa Valley. Our destination was Baalbek—a fantastic ancient temple complex smack in the middle of Lebanon. Until the mid-70s, Baalbek had been the scene of a yearly pageant, and Lebanese would get misty-eyed when they talked of driving out of Beirut and watching the dancing and singing in pagan temples bathed with colored lights.

On our way up the Lebanon Mountains toward Baalbek, Abed stopped at a forlorn coffee and souvenir shop. We poked around and finally bought some trinkets and sipped a soda. As we drove away, Abed told us:

"The man say-ed to me, 'Oh, I am very happy. The American tourists are coming back, inshallah.' He wantis this very much."

So did we. But, O Lebanon . . . you are such an enchanting country, so benign in climate, so exotic in landscape—but so fractured and self-devouring with your wretched refugee camps, hundred-year-old grudges, explosions in the night.

With Abed, we wound our way down the Lebanon Mountains and into the Bekaa, traveling the route caravans had followed for centuries. Just south of the temples we let a shopkeeper talk us into buying several "certified" artifacts from her dusty shelves. An ancient perfume vase was one. We knew that the vase had to be a fake—but it seemed appropriate to own a piece of possibly genuine, possibly *faux* Lebanon.

After wandering around deserted temples, we drove to a little park, through which a clear mountain stream gurgled. Abed opened his trunk and produced little Lebanese pizzas covered with pine nuts; his wife had made these for us the night before.

At such times, I think, one cannot help but hear heartbreaking echoes of Lebanon's Khalil Gibran in the brook, the swooshing cedars, the smiles of the Lebanese—"as in yonder valley the myrtle breathes its fragrance into space. Through the hands of such as these, God speaks, and from behind their eyes he smiles upon the earth."

But too seldom. Too seldom.

Two years later, the violence welled up into war. A year after that, in a burst of false hope, I even heard the Commodore pianist playing "I'm a Yankee Doodle Dandy" to a contingent of US Marine officers. But the violence never left Lebanon.

Now, four years later, even those days seem halcyon.

We accidently broke the perfume vase a year ago. Baalbek, where Abed so calmly drove us, is where many of the American hostages have been held by their captors. And, finally, in another spasm of civil war, the Commodore itself was shattered and looted in February. Abed no longer waits at the corner with his big white Pontiac, ready to drive journalists around his country.

Being a journalist, I could sit here and tell you reasons behind all the awfulness, all the kidnapping, all the fighting. But that would be what the head says about Lebanon. What the heart says is different. It prays that one day that souvenir dealer will have his wish, that the land of milk and honey will reopen to innocent tourists, and the myrtle will breathe its fragrance for those who love peace, not war. 🐚

TRIO FROM LATIN AMERICA:
FAREWELL TO AGUA ZARCA
Harry Lee Little

All those years—nearly ten in truth—the village had been there, some vague two hours, two and a half hours, some three hours from our homestead in the Mexican Rain Forest. ❧ Although Jan and Becca had been there many times, I had never attempted the hike they described, depending upon the season, as "tough," "horrible," or "impossible." ❧ I understood well enough what they meant, having much earlier served my own apprenticeship to jungle trailing in all seasons, but my sense of the actual distance remained vague. ❧

Our realization that we had an entire village for neighbors came abruptly one mid-morning when in our lonely virgin vale we heard voices, a whole parcel of Man Fridays, and up at the cave where before we had heard only the chattering and scolding of our numerous spider monkeys. These latter had resented our invasion of what had been perhaps for some centuries *their* virgin vale. These new voices were not scolding, and they were the voices of men. Like Robinson Crusoe on his lonely island, we shuddered with our very mixed feelings. Men, a band of men, where we had no cause to believe men had walked for centuries. Where did they come from? What were they doing? What should we do?

Shortly after our arrival in the vale, many months before, Becca had seen a Lacandon Indian crossing just below our camp. Could there be, then, a little group of "lost" Lacandones living up here at the foot of the mountains?

We listened. Their voices were louder than Lacandones ever spoke when out hunting. Should we reveal our presence? Their behavior clearly showed they were unaware of us.

I shouted. They stopped talking. "Come on down here," I called in Spanish. We could hear muffled discussion. At last they began to come out of the jungle into the little clearing where our hut stood. Soon there were ten or more, all adult men, all who more or less understood Spanish. One attractive, intelligent, volatile youth was their spokesman.

While the others recovered from their astonishment at finding a blond, pale-faced family of Crusoes in the middle of the virgin jungle, he explained who they were: Tzeltales or Highland Mayas who had abandoned worn-out and dried-out corn fields to seek virgin lands. We had, it was clear, been neighbors for over a year.

They came to work, they sent—for a short time—twenty or more of their children to the school Becca and I opened at the request of two of their youths. In time some became dear friends, others came only to work, some few returned for one reason or another to the Highlands.

Then one day we saw we had been discovered by other neighbors, neighbors from another direction—bad neighbors. They were also from the Highlands and had come down for similar reasons, worn-out, dried-out because burned-out, lands. But these were not Indians. They were direct descendents of the old Conquistadores. And they still saw themselves in the Conquistador role, that is, as the Indians' masters by right of conquest. We, by becoming the Indians' friends and benefactors, were traitors and enemies. Slowly they had forced us into an untenable position, an easy feat for bad neighbors. Just how easy I had never realized. We would have to give up everything and seek a new life in a new land with good neighbors, or no neighbors.

All but a very few of Agua Zarca's hundred or more people were sad and tried to persuade us to stay on, but gradually most admitted the impossibility, knowing well that they themselves were able to withstand the "conquerors" only by their numbers, not by law.

Departure Day. For half an hour we had to watch the two elements tearing our house apart, the Indians and the serfs of the conquerors as they vied for every scrap of goods, even the rags, we had to leave behind. But as quickly as possible we turned our backs and headed out over the trail to Agua Zarca, I for the first time, and into a world I had only read about for over ten years.

Some of the youths had recently opened a new trail from the village.

"This is a big improvement," Jan and Becca agreed. Happily the Dry Season had set in.

"Not bad," I said, but little Rima, our little orphaned spider monkey in her sling over my shoulder, did not like it, and Smoky, the Belgian police dog, kept close to Jan's heels.

Our friends from Agua Zarca carrying the incredible amount of stuff we had decided to take, books and clothes, strung out ahead of us. Chan Bor and Na Bora, the only Lacandones to see us off, followed close behind. At first the virgin jungle, then grown over clearings, then pig tracks and wallows, then pigs . . . At last, after about two hours, we spotted the village, beautifully situated upon a plateau between a clear flowing creek and the broad Jatate River.

Pedro helped us across the creek. We passed slowly through the village and on to the airstrip down by the river. Beautiful Agua Zarca! They greeted us, old familiar faces, each from a little compound fortress, for the village is shared with the swine, and all the beauty is blighted, desecrated by the swine. Why am I sorrowful at this my first and very likely my last view of Agua Zarca? Have I not walked through such villages a hundred times? But the faces then, in my pioneer days, were not the faces of dearly loved neighbors.

Two days and two nights "waiting for the plane," but the cool, green river is handy, the airstrip is a vast playground for children—no hogs. Here at least for safety's sake they are fenced off.

There are many generous offers of food . . . In spite of which or because of which we suddenly become self aware of our role as qualified refugees. Rima alone is able to lose herself in play. The children have her for the first time all to themselves and she has all of them to herself . . . And I for the first and the last time, can see the full range of mountains and our homestead site nestled at their feet from the vantage of Agua Zarca.

At last the plane, the plane that admits only the hastiest of farewells— there lies Agua Zarca only a couple of hundred feet below. It is bare and blighted still, but in another moment or two of swift flight, only the little thatch huts stand out, and in each doorway if we shut our eyes we can see the warm, familiar, and friendly faces of our good neighbors—none better in the world, the Mexican Indian. ❧

Trio From Latin America: Nothing—Or A Great Something

Jan Little

The woman is kind to receive us so graciously as strangers. ❦ Every hotel is filled so we ask for hospitality at the mission. ❦ For these few minutes of our acquaintanceship we chat easily enough. ❦ We recognize one another without saying so, because we've received similar schooling, been tutored in the common graces, and in education to the highest truths given mankind. ❦ But she is puzzled. Her question is simple enough, many have asked us the same: "Why do you wish to live so remotely?" ❦

If a model were made of our delights, our interests and our goals, I am sure a computer would furnish in a matter of seconds what we have been years working out. Starting with a desire to live with the wildlife unthreatened and still unaware of predatory man with bow and arrow, blow pipe or gun, to plant and husband a plot of ground unthreatened by cattle ranching or plantation agriculture with its villages of half starved laborers—wanting this plot, which we call a homestead, to be in the Tropic Zone amid the fullest bloom of the vegetable kingdom and situated upon a mountain slope—all this seemed to result in the location "no one has ever heard of . . ."

But I think I understand what is troubling the woman. And merely to explain why we want the wilderness will not satisfy her. To explain the factors making for remoteness is not enough. Her own life has been lived remote from the world of actual civilized life, but possession of a radio plus access to an airplane seems to her a partial explanation for her venturing so far afield: What really bothers her is the confrontation with the "Nothing."

This "Nothing" is pointed out with an expansive sweep of the hand indicating quite a bit of the earth. Someone says, "Out there is 'Nothing.'" The implication is that humankind cannot live with this "Nothing."

Primitive and peasant peoples who have lived next door to a wilderness imaginatively make it "Something," the haunt of creatures allied to humans, giants, fairies, trolls, elves, demons, spirits or even gods and goddesses. We may smile at such fancies now; the earth has less wilderness today, rather it is become the precincts of petroleum, gold, uranium, timber, and animals to be hunted for one motive or another.

But my friend is pensive and she can understand that there is something for us in this "Nothing." For Harry, my husband, who is a field naturalist, is forever appearing a fantasy of bird life, a ballet of forest creatures, a perpetual pageant of intimated forms and moods and designs. For Rebecca my daughter there are the creeks and the flowers, especially the shy, exquisite orchids, creation at its fount. For me, there is the realm of plants growing so vibrantly that foresters speak of this profusion as "story and understory" as though speaking of the different levels within a building. It is vitality without seasonal stop or slowness, a realm still unknown, still unrealized and unhusbanded in its potential for fruition.

This is all understandable to her who has come out of a culture that has many plants called into being from a primitive state. What bothers her is that to *live* for such rewards one must confront aloneness.

It is not an aloneness we deliberately choose, and few there are who do. We simply have not been joined by others who share similar motivations— with desire enough to persist in the effort of achievement.

This aloneness is very difficult and even unpleasant for one strange reason—the presence of oneself. There are here no easy distractions, no ready identification with other persons in their activities or moods, and small are the comforts provided by other than one's own hands.

This loosening process can be fascinating, even startling in a detached manner of observance. Like seeing still another underlying layer of wallpaper in the renovation of an old house. Or hearing "voices"! For weeks old radio commercials rang in my head. I had never realized how much verbal baggage from my childhood, listening to radio programs, was still being carried around. Whatever this stripping process means, it does not end as an ending. Like the seed coat through which the plant has thrust its growing root and leaf, it is scarcely noticeable and little lamented. And like the plant which has many a brave adventure ahead, one forgets that aloneness back there in the darkness for now is the time of living in the well-watered garden, home to the ever-toiling earthworm, the ever-mischievous monkey and all those who build in the old waste places. ❧

191

Trio From Latin America:
Pioneers In A New Wilderness
Harry Lee Little

"Ike got discouraged and Betsy got mad, And the dog wagged his tail And looked wonderfully sad—" U.S.A. folk song ∝

I speak of pioneering in the old specific meaning of a family or families, or even an individual, going forth to a geographical frontier to seek a fresh start by carving a home and hearth out of the wilderness. As there are so few such wildernesses left on earth most people assume this kind of pioneering is no longer being done. Not so. In places such as the Guiana Highlands and the Amazon Basin, in South America, it is still possible to pioneer in this ancient special sense. If few are doing so it is not so much from the lack of land as the lack of incentive.

Incentive? What makes a pioneer? School children learn that the quest for religious freedom is a prime cause—or political persecution. Though Daniel Boone hardly qualifies in these cases, yet the children also learn that Daniel was in some ways a typical pioneer. I myself have preferred to find inspiration or incentive in those nameless homeseekers such as "Ike" and "Betsy" and all of those of my forefathers who, in covered sleds, in the depth of winter, penetrated "The Wilderness," as the Amerindians called what is now Vermont. There are also those Austrian mountaineers who voyaged around the Horn in the 1800s to settle in a remote Peruvian Andean valley rather than see their children forced to migrate to cities; or those unidentified Brazilians who somehow found the courage to abandon their homes in the drought-seared Sertao region of the East Coast to voyage thousands of winding swamp river miles into the eastern foothills of the Andes. And for a final inspiring example we have the miracle of modern Israel whose pioneers cleared and drained and planted the malarial swamps of the Upper Jordan.

All of these nameless pioneers of the past now help to sustain Jan and Becca and me as we sharpen our machetes and begin literally to carve a home

192

and hearth out of the wilds of the Guiana Highland in the extreme north-western part of Brazil.

The problems remain the same, mainly how to subsist while planting and building. Here—as yet—we have no Indians, friendly or unfriendly. We are alone some five days by motorboat from the nearest general store and post office. And we can be reached by dugout canoe only at certain seasons of high water. This isolation is because there is no other way to get beyond those regions which are regularly visited by hunters and fishermen. Unlike Daniel Boone and other pioneers we do not hunt. All our food has to be brought in, a severe limitation but we are writing Naturalists as well as pioneers and need Nature undisturbed.

What have we found? Thus far it is merely a toehold in the foothills where the Guiana Highlands spill over into Brazil. Here with the Amazonian swamps stretching hundreds of miles to the south and west we came to a ridge of outcropping white quartz with mountains of Andean majesty a few miles to the northeast. Although our homestead may not be a thousand feet above sea level these mountains bless us with an ever moist and ever cool climate that makes hard work a special pleasure after listless months in the steaming lowlands of the Rio Negro.

And lest quartz ridges sound inhospitable let me mention that our new home includes a wall of quartz ledge which at the hearth site provides a fireplace over seven feet tall and five feet wide. Quartz sometimes contains gold. As yet we've found none but already we find a foretaste of that blessed peace and contentment not even gold can be sure to bring. 🐚

AMBLING
Joyce Grenfell

What do you do with an unexpected gift of unplanned time? ❧ We found ourselves with a beautifully empty engagement book where we had thought to find it full and spilling over. ❧ Of course we didn't go to the art galleries and concerts we'd always said we would go to if only we had the time; nor did we read the whole of Tolstoy. ❧ One of the things we did do, though, was to amble and discover, slowly and on foot, the back streets of our London "village." ❧

Like New York, London is made up of hundreds of small "villages" where the locals shop and post mail and get the dry cleaning done. (It was in my temporary "village" in New York near Seventh Avenue and West 55th Street that I learned to say "Hi" instead of "Good morning"; and where I met the delights of Horn & Hardardt's. At the time I was appearing in a show at the little Bijou Theater, and I often ate at H and H where the girls behind the counter became my friends and so did Bob, an ex-pianist, who ran the cash desk and took an interest in The Theater.)

Our London "village," that is the shopping area, is about 500 yards long; there you can get most of the daily necessities and extra luxuries at our delicatessen—the things you can no longer get in our "village" are a spool of thread, a button, or any other such vital needs. Do fewer people need buttons and thread? They get harder to track down, although the next village five minutes walk away up in the Kings Road area still has one shop where they sell these things in a few basic but unsuitable colors.

Needless to say I am fully familiar with our village shops, but what I didn't know at all well, until our unplanned ambling time, were the small

194

side streets behind the main road, many with early 19th-century houses with little gardens front and back, window boxes and sometimes even a tree. Many of these houses have only six rooms on three floors; the bigger ones are mostly converted into flats. All have flowers somewhere.

The month that was unexpectedly bestowed on us was in summer, when the gardens were exuberant. One Regency house, freshly painted dazzling white, appeared to be rising out of a ruffled petticoat of petunias. They were planted in tubs so close together that you might have thought they were in a raised flower bed. White flowers predominated, and were set off by a few striped red and white ones, and there were pinks and reds, purples and pale mauves—it was a veritable explosion of petunias.

In the ordinary way I am always en route somewhere, with a fixed time of arrival at the other end of the journey, so I take the main roads because they are the quickest way. That's why I didn't know the side streets very well. Ambling means you don't have to be anywhere particular at any special time, so I pause to look at gardens and grapevines—yes, grapevines—in London. They grow well here and climb up drainpipes to the tiny wrought-iron balconies that are too delicate for an adult to step out onto but nevertheless qualify as balconies because they are there to prevent anyone walking out of the upstairs French windows into space.

I also pause to speak to an occasional cat.

I must declare that I am not a cat woman. If I lived in the country again I would like to have a dog, but though cats and I are tolerant of each other there is no natural bond between us. Among other things, I don't like being sprung upon even though I can admire the leap. But a cat met on an amble tends to stay on the ground and rub against what it assumes must be a friendly leg and this is flattering and can be endured.

Midmorning is a good time for encountering cats in relaxed mood. It is a relaxed time when those with time to spare are abroad in the quiet streets. Pre-school children are to be seen riding their tricycles up and down small paths in tiny front gardens, skillfully turning at high speed in almost no space at all, pretending they are motorbikes and making motorbike noises with their mouths. Sometimes the children come to the front gate and tell you their names and the names of their brother and or sister, and of their cat. They tell you what they did yesterday and what they can do now that they've got you there as a captive audience. Would we like to see them ride their tricycles? Child-watching is a ploy I like, so I say yes.

Once when we were in Australia we met a three-year-old called Simon

195

who had just mastered the art of hopping. It is a great moment when you find you can travel on one leg, and Simon was aflame with the success of it. We are contemporaries of his grandparents, with whom we were staying, so you will understand how pleased I was when Simon fell in love with me. There was one slight flaw: He believed I was my husband's mother.

After breakfast he would say to my husband, "Shall we go and see your mother?" and together they visited me in my room where I was writing letters after having had my breakfast in bed.

"Hullo," said Simon, already standing on one foot and then, for my delight, offering me his rarest jewel:

"Would you like to see me hop?"

"Oh *yes*," I said encouragingly. With infinite concentration and heavy breathing he remembered how to do it and jerked his way across the room, fair hair bouncing on his forehead, his face growing rosy with his effort.

"Well done," I said, ready to get back to my letter writing.

"Would you like to see me hop again?"

"Well—yes, of course."

It could have turned into perpetual motion if my husband hadn't suggested a walk in the garden; because Simon, back at the starting point, once more wondered if I would like to see him hop back *again* and, to be frank, you do get to the end of hopping fairly soon when you are only the watcher.

The tempo of life at midmorning in the shaded side streets of our London "village" is delightfully *lento*. You seldom see anyone hurrying. Housewives can be seen moving about in upstairs rooms, dusting perhaps, but they have time to come to the window and look out to make sure the street is still there. Some are already in the garden-level kitchen starting to prepare the midday meal. Babies, put out into their perambulators to sleep, don't always nod off at once and you can hear them talking in gurgles as they discover their fingers and toes. You can also hear music from a piano somewhere, or is it a radio? Retired citizens are out ambling as we are, and there is time to smile and mention the weather and the garden we are admiring; time as W. H. Davies wrote, "to stand and stare."

Back in the "village" the pace quickens—we stand in line to buy zucchini and peaches.

"Keeping you busy these days?" enquires Arthur at the fruiterers.

"No, I'm just ambling."

"Lovely," he says.

I agree. ❧

196

THE VOICE OF A FRIEND
Doris Peel

One morning in London (this was years ago) an incident was reported on the BBC News. ✍ The previous evening, in an area marked at the time by an alarming increase in racial disturbances, a crippled Asian had been set upon by a gang of youths rowdily emerging from a local pub. ✍ A passing-by young man had come to his rescue. ✍ And had himself—before the police could arrive—been so severely beaten up that his condition in a hospital was reported to be "critical." ✍

Within the same hour I had a telephone call: from someone who, among intimates, was apt to ring early before her own exceptionally full days began.

"You heard, didn't you? I found the hospital where he is, and have just been speaking with the doctor in charge. He's a clerk, a junior bank clerk, and physically slight, so must have known he'd nothing to depend on *that* way. . . . I'm having flowers sent, and a note they can read to him when he comes around. You write one too, it can be taken with mine." Then, characteristically, "He mustn't even for a moment be allowed to think of dying! That's what we can tell him. *'You are needed here, dear boy!* All of us need you—'"

That evening there was a follow-up item on the News. The young man had regained consciousness. Cautious hope was expressed.

My friend had a name both famous and loved. It can still, and instantly, evoke warm affection in all manner of companies, even though almost five years have passed since so many of us came together to bid her farewell at "A Service of Thanksgiving" in Westminster Abbey.

On that wintry afternoon—among those formally escorted to seats

197

in the Quire Stalls—there were numerous faces familiar to the British public at large. Later one was to learn that out beyond the screen every pew was packed by members of that public, well before the chamber-orchestra Prelude had drawn to a close with Bach's "Sheep may safely graze." Toward the end of the Service came what so often (this being England) has sounded out on ceremonial occasions. The words of John Bunyan. From "Pilgrim's Progress":

> *After this it was noised abroad, that Mr.* Valiant-for-truth *was taken with a summons. . . . When he understood it, he called for his Friends, and told them of it. Then said he, I am going to my Fathers. When the Day that he must go hence, was come, many accompanied him to the River side, into which, as he went, he said,* Death, where is thy Sting? *And as he went down deeper, he said,* Grave, where is thy Victory? *So he passed over, and all the Trumpets sounded for him on the other side.*

A company of friends, that afternoon. Variously making its way by limousine and taxi, Underground and bus, to take part like this in a glorious welling-up of what she herself had always so delighted in. The music, the poetry . . . and now by implication the tributes to a faith held to through a long career, so blithely spanning such a diversity of accomplishments and continuing in full fettle until she left.

A motley company, as assuredly she'd have wished.

Perhaps including a former junior clerk in a bank, remembering a letter that once came to him out of the blue. And even—why not?—a certain old street-cleaner, tidied up to pay *his* respects.

I was walking home with her that day, when suddenly as we turned off the King's Road, a character bundled up in an assortment of woolies stopped short with his whiskery broom suspended. The next instant, his free arm had shot forward.

Accusingly pointing a forefinger, he said, "Proper caught out *you* were last night!"

Quick as a flash, she demanded, "Did you know the answer?"

"Never 'eard of 'im," he said. (Bartok it had been.)

"But *you're* on the telly! You're supposed to!"

Sounding severe as a nanny, he was grinning delightedly. Both of them were.

"What's your name?" she asked.

"Alf," he said.

"Well look here, Alf, you'd better keep an eye on me! Mustn't overdo the clowning, must I?" Then, as if it mattered, "How'd you like my new dress?"

Planted there in the gutter, he appeared to ponder this. "Pinkie, weren't it?"

"Perhaps—just perhaps—a bit too girlish?" She waited attentively, while he took his time.

Then as if the two of them were cozily on their own, under quite other circumstances—"You'll do," he told her.

The program they'd been referring to—although highly rated among television series, both for its lightly worn learning in music matters and the wit and affectionate interplay among the distinguished panelists—I must say I'd never thought of as natural fare for an old chap sweeping a Chelsea street. But then, of course, it had had on it since first launched someone who—as we were now about to move on—could cavalierly toss back over a half-turned shoulder, "And, you Alf! *You'll* do too!"

A reciprocating salute! And delivered with full style.

Several springs ago I was back in Jerusalem. And someone first known there as a very young man at once came to the Hospice where I was again staying.

While we were having tea in the high-walled courtyard, with the oleander and bougainvillea blazingly in bloom, David—headman of the household staff—came out to announce a long-distance call. A rather lengthy one, it proved. And when I reemerged, it was to find Khalil hunched over a transistor radio.

My arrival had coincided with the invasion of Lebanon. And among all the friends being seen again—Israeli and Arab, on both sides of the city—a striking number seemed to hang on the BBC World Service for the only news reports they were prepared to credit. But this wasn't a usual hour for news. Instead, and startlingly, a voice was speaking. Then a laugh rang out: buoyant, unmistakable. Still another replay, from her familiar repertoire.

Khalil had looked up quickly. "*It's her!* Your friend!"

Momentarily I was nonplussed. How on earth—

Then everything snapped together. Starting with that first arrival, years before, in a Jerusalem where one had expected to stay three weeks but had, instead, been pitched headlong into the full aftermath of the Six Day War. Which meant witnessing both the soaring euphoria of the victors (who might have been led by Joshua himself) and the shock and humiliation of the utterly defeated.

199

On the losing side were numbers of university students. At the time returned home for the start of their summer holidays, they were to find themselves—almost overnight, it seemed—not only in territories henceforth to remain "occupied" but drastically cut off from their studies in Cairo and Beirut and Amman. And this in a society where higher education was the sesame-key to any opening up of their lives.

Khalil was among them: though set apart, when first met, by a reticence so extreme that only by scrupulously honoring it was one gradually to be accepted. Then when we were alone, suddenly he could say things like, "To die of a broken heart, this I now understand."

"Ah, but surely not for you! You can't mean that."

"Why do you speak angrily?"

"It's not anger, Khalil. It's this feeling I have—that you're going to be greatly needed, in whatever lies ahead."

"But you don't understand! What am I to belong to? When I can't even feel what I'm supposed to feel—"

Not the rampant despair, but the terrible bitterness, the hatred, I took him to mean.

And he said then, as if speaking nakedly from some literal limbo, "I know now I can never kill. Do you see what this means? *How can anything be loved without hating what will destroy it?*"

That deadliest of equations. Millennia-old.

But even then, I suppose, one must have trusted his own capacity to wrestle with the angel. And later on, at a rendezvous arranged with great discretion—between four young Arabs one was prepared to vouch for and a group of young Israelis equally known and trusted—it was Khalil's voice that suddenly at a crucial moment made itself heard through the clash of other voices. "Listen to us! Just *listen!* As Arab, as Jew—are we still—still—to go on failing as our fathers have failed before us?"

The voice had trembled. He was the youngest one present.

It was very late, after midnight, when we drove up from the coastal kibbutz through the now-dense silence of the Judean hills, toward a city that can still evoke that long-ago cry *"O Jerusalem, Jerusalem—"* Overhead in a vast and velvety sky were the same stars once looked up to from desert and mount and shepherded field.

"Khalil—"

"Yes?"

200

We'd spoken softly, sharing the back of the borrowed Land Rover.

"Can you hear them? The stars."

His head turned, tilted upward.

"Isn't it a kind of singing, that's now begun?"

For him, I meant.

Now these years later, in a courtyard again blooming with its oleander and bougainvillea, he was completing for me an episode I'd not known about in full.

"The telephone numbers, you'll remember them?"

After a moment I remembered. When eventually one had had to return to London, two telephone numbers had been left behind. At either of them, my current whereabouts would always be known—this in case any of the students actually managed to get to England at a period when so many ardently longed to do so.

By something of a miracle, Khalil himself had turned up, and at once from the airport had telephoned as instructed. Only to learn that the previous week I had left for Poland.

"It was a terrible disappointment! I'd *depended on you* being there!" (No point in saying, "Why on earth didn't you get in touch before you came?"— his own society, alas, being one hardly noted for humdrum practicalities.) "It must have shown, the disappointment, because she—the voice—said 'What a pity!' She wanted to know who I was and where I'd come from and how we'd met. She asked many questions, then told me to ring again at another hour."

When he did so, she'd typically—and bossily—taken charge. Someone known to her had once held an official post in what was then called Palestine, under the British Mandate. Now he had a grandson of Khalil's age who had himself proposed sharing his student room in Bloomsbury while a further arrangement was being sorted out. The following morning a pair of theater tickets arrived in the mail, with a personal note instructing the two young men to present themselves in her dressing-room after the performance.

"There were other people already there, all talking and laughing. . . . She was like a tall queen, I thought, in a long dress very beautiful, and we just stood there by the door, too shy to go inside. Until suddenly she came over to us, and said, 'Hullo, you two! I'm so pleased you could come.'"

But it was something she said when they were about to leave that evidently had taken special root. "You see, Khalil, if we've the faith to step out

201

into this world as a friend, then friendship can come to meet us in all sorts of ways."

Spoken to a young man born into so heartbreakingly difficult a place—and years before he was to prove himself in a mediator role that may never be blazed across a world's press, but all the time, like a candle, can be emitting who knows how quenchless a light?

In the courtyard he said, "I never saw her again. But I still remember her as someone—" here he paused for a moment—"who wouldn't ever want another person to feel shut out." ◥

A SAMPLING
OF SONNETS

A Sampling Of Sonnets

A sonnet is a fourteen-line poem following one of several fixed verse and rhyme schemes, usually in rhymed iambic pentameter, usually exploring a single theme and enforcing certain disciplines on the poet. Home Forum publishes a number of them every year.

In an essay about sonnets Paul O. Williams wrote: "Surely its originators had no idea what they had accomplished in creating a poem that would survive the disappearance of almost all the other forms of the time (the 13th century), would spread throughout Western literature, and would become a form on which many great poets have lavished attention . . .

"But sonnets have not been universally admired, even among people who have written them. In our time, with its love of poetic freedom, new sonnets are often, even generally, seen as fripperies or exercises . . .

"The writer of sonnets is challenged. Not only does the sonnet make formal demands, but somehow it expects a solid content, a serious discussion, tightly structured yet lyrical. A light observation cannot easily be stretched into the form—the result is merely a verbal curlicue. A complex subject tends to strain its seams with unstated implications. And yet earnestness is what the sonnet expects.

"Good sonnets tend to be understated without seeming to be. They growl in dulcet tones, say deeply essential things in the voice of someone ordering a light dessert, or batter against the form while taking care not to break it."

In a Roots of Poems essay commenting on a sonnet she had written, Doris Kerns Quinn said: "I am a list-maker, and some days I put 'write a poem' on my list. Then I sit in my armchair next to the window and try to think of something. More correctly speaking, I listen . . .

"At such times writing in the sonnet form seems to help, so on this occasion I started thinking in iambic pentameters. After a time, the first line came . . . In an hour or so I had the poem, and after a few days—during which I made minor changes—it was ready to journey out into the world."

Here are a sampling of sonnets which have journeyed out into the world and found a home at the Home Forum. 🐚

205

THE TRUMPETER OF KRAKOW
Robert C. Jones

Cold. Through Florian's Gate—a Tartar wind.
Roses and snowflakes in the market square:
Flower stall roofs, red and yellow blooms.
Count the hour. Ten. Now: The window opens,
exposes the trumpet's bell. Wait. And movement
slows as eyes look up. Mary's Cathedral tower
lifts dark against the snow. Brass notes shower
down. In mid-flight: Stop. The window closes.
The flower woman counts each blossom twice.
Counts wrinkled zlotys twice into my hands.
Looks at us from the corners of her eyes.
Across the Vistula, Wawel Church stands.
There, Great Sigismund's bell once filled the skies—
with doom or joy. The drifting snowflakes rise.

SINK SLOWLY, VENICE
Doris Kerns Quinn

"Venice is slowly sinking into the sea."—News Item

Sink slowly, Venice, for I may come late;
Retard your amber for an afternoon;
Resist the downward pull and stay afloat
One night beneath a gondola-shaped moon.
For I will come, I will not tarry long,
And you'll be all you promised me you'd be—
A golden city, dreamlike, softly hung
Somewhere between the heaven and the sea.
I shall not need a week, a month, a year—
One afternoon, one night on your canals,
One golden song sung by a gondolier
While water laps against the fabled walls
Is all I'll ask you from your gracious wait.
Sink slowly, Venice, for I may come late.

DIMENSIONS IN PASSAGE
E.O. Staley

Ours were giant fathers! How we'd skip
along beside their knees or feel the ground
tremble, shaken by the rumbling sound
of hearty laughter at a neighbor's quip.
Or did *we* tremble? Which? Listening thus
to these enormous creatures it was worth
childish terror, knowing they owned the earth
whose giant acres they'd hand down to us.

As we grew older, the earth grew smaller;
ponds became puddles. We suspected then
that fathers were a tribe of shrinking men.
We stretched up eager arms, grew no taller
than giants resting, pennies on their eyes,
in acres scaled exactly to our size.

CHICHEN ITZA:
SACRED CITY OF THE MAYA
Anne Marx

Diary Page of January 29, 1988

We roam these ruins as we try to trace
the lives of those who piled preposterous stone
on stone for temples to exalt their own
existence, castles and pyramids to face
us eerily, stilled now the furious pace
once prevalent here. In science, they outshone
their world, practicing skills so far unknown—
yet time long made mere remnants of their race.

Back at the castle that we call hotel,
a splendor savored by the present cast,
like Mayan men sure of supremacy
within their City by the Sacred Well,
we wince at warnings conjured from a past
much like our own vainglorious century.

THE UNICYCLIST
Donald Bailey

Kind are late shadows after summer rain
as Joan and Barbara storm the misty lane,
riding their bicycles in a bold display:
emperors are not more confident than they
nor wings more swift. Our bikers pass the row,
impatient now to meet that boy they know.
Light streams across the way, ah who rides there?
Elaine of Astolat was not more fair
nor queeens more brave. Who rides on one lone wheel,
erect and golden-haired? Her eyes conceal
resistless will to hold her wheel on course,
untroubled by the friends who might endorse
newer and safer ways to explore the lane.
Kind sunbeams linger: these and love remain.

ESTHWAITE WATER
A.L. Hendriks

From Ravenglass to Wreay each onyx lake
Is held a jewel ringed by cloistered trees;
Yet all are tranquil tideless land-lipped seas
Upon whose shores no strident combers break.
It opens wide, this unastonished land
Accustomed to accept the stranger's eyes,
To tell how stone and water glide and rise
And mingle at the tarn's beach where we stand.
We sense their silent music on a strand
Or ragged sedge; nearby, calm cattle sleep
Not minding whether fells are cold or steep,
Embraced by love assured, and firm, and planned.
All Nature's poems made by perfect mind
Are clearly wrought; nor are they left unsigned.

WINTER MEETING—A CHRISTMAS SONNET
Paul O. Williams

The wind is wrong. The dog is not aware
a buck is watching us through standing corn.
His tawny coat is earth, his glinting pair
of antlers seem more ragged stalk-ends, torn
by harvesting. I see his silent stare
at us as though from tense and floating eyes.
Oh, he is fully there—and yet not there:
like Christmas thoughts, I muse, which can arise
in any field, at any time, confer
the resource of their being on the scene.
Once born to men, the thoughts of Christ occur
unasked, bestow their implications. Clean
and deep, desired or not, they offer grace.
From then till now there is no empty place.

Andreae, Christopher: "Art to Stumble Over" 11/28/88

Austin, April: "Singing Verdi's Requiem in Concert" 7/13/88

Bailey, Donald: "The Unicyclist" (sonnet) 5/16/88

Bambery, Jane Brown: "Tale of a Tea Bowl" 1/26/89

Berkman, Ted: "Learning Where to Start" 6/2/82

Bond, Ruskin: "From Small Beginnings" 9/21/82

Brantsen, Jeremy: "An American on Kosygin Street" 9/14/87

Brown, Elizabeth: "Jogging in Japan" 8/17/88

Buckmaster, Henrietta: "Freedom and Lessons in Fortitude" 2/18/82

Candlin, Enid Saunders: "A Musical Education in Shanghai" (published as "As You Dream") 3/17/71

Canham, Patience: "Something She May Not Have Known Before" 7/22/75

Carlson, Susan: "An Interview with Sculptor George Rickey" (published as "Balancing Art To The Gram" and "Blades That Draw On The Wind") 12/19/88 and 12/20/88

Comstock, Jim: "A Farewell Gift" (published as "What Could I Give Her When She Went to College?") 4/10/84

DeVries, Hilary: "Americans in Paris, or, Are We Having Fun Yet?" 8/3/88

Dresser, Cynthia: "Music in the Air: Immigrants Learn English in a Post Office" 8/30/88

Giordan, Alma Roberts: "Split Green Vases" 7/15/87

Gould, John: "Swill" (published as "Scraps Make Swell Swill") 11/25/88

Graham, Virginia: "Nature Study" (published under the byline Virginia Thesiger) 9/26/70

Grenfell, Joyce: "Ambling" 12/5/73

Hasselstrom, Linda: "South Dakota Night" 3/24/88

Hendriks, A. L.: "Esthwaite Water" (sonnet) 11/9/88

Highwater, Jamake: " 'Who Can Tell the Dancer from the Dance' " 10/5/88

Holmstrom, David: "Silence" 7/6/66

Huey, Michael: "An Interview with Painter Wolf Kahn" 12/12/88

Hunter, Frederic: "The Terrace" 6/27/68

Hunter, Paul: "The Bird of Paradise Corsage" (published as "About a Corsage") 11/19/74

Jones, Robert C.: "The Trumpeter of Krakow" (sonnet; published as "The Trumpeter of Krakov") 1/24/89

Kidder, Rushworth: "The Raccoon Shrugged" 9/17/85

LePelley, Guernsey: "The Cat Who Ate Spaghetti, The Dog Who Chased Cows" 8/23/88

Lewis, Maggie: "Into the Hearts of Thousands" 5/14/79

Little, Harry Lee: "A Trio from Latin America" (part one of the trio published as "Farewell to Aqua Zarca" 8/29/73; part three as "Pioneers in a New Wilderness" 8/2/76)

Little, Jan: "A Trio from Latin America" (second part of the trio published as "Nothing—Or A Great Something") 6/23/75

Lofthouse, Norma: "A Garden Party with Chagall" 4/25/88

Manuel, Diane: "Animal Crackers in My Purse" 9/1/87

Marx, Anne: "Chichen Itza: Sacred City of the Maya" (sonnet) 11/22/88

Mayes, Dennis: "Alice and the Yellow Leaves" 10/20/88

Mazel, David: "A Letter to My Father" 10/4/88

McBride, Bunny: "Mercy's Greeting" 3/31/82

Millar, Neil: "On Humor" (published as "When We Take Ourselves Too Solemnly") 5/24/78

Noble, Alex: "Three Short Musings" (published separately as "Decisions Before Their Time" 7/6/79; "Right For Me" 9/11/79; "Taking Another Approach") 10/19/79

Nordell, Roderick: "Rich, Buddy" 8/22/70

Nyerges, Christopher: "Homelessness: One Man's Story" 4/20/88

Palakeel, Thomas: "Dreams of Elephants" 2/8/89

Paton, Alan: "A Writer's Reflections" 10/3/83

Peel, Doris: "The Voice of a Friend" 3/20/86

Pradervand, Pierre: "Asking, Loving" 10/7/82

Quinn, Doris Kerns: "The Crown Joodles, the Mysteries of Egg-pit, and Other Joys of Being a Mispronunciation Expert" 9/21/87; "Sink Slowly, Venice" (sonnet) 3/23/85

Ritchie, Elisavietta: "We Are All Only Visiting" (published as "All Creatures Great and Small") 10/30/78

Rottmann, Larry: "From a Diary of a Veteran Returning to Vietnam" (published as "From a Diary of a Veteran on a Trip Back to Vietnam") 11/10/88

Siepel, Kevin: "Strangers on a Train" (published as "Falling in Love on a Train") 7/5/88

Simmons, Tom: "Night Landings" 4/27/88

Staley, E. O.: "Dimensions in Passage" (sonnet) 4/5/88

Stone, Darren: "A Christmas Lesson" (published as "A Piano for Christmas") 12/22/61

Stromholt, Hallett: " 'Hour-dogging' in Montana" 9/15/88

Stuart, Pippa: "I'd Like to Make You a Chair" 12/24/86

Theroux, Paul: "Winter in Africa" 7/2/65

Thomas, Owen: "Joy from an Infant Planet" 8/12/87

Tiberghien, Susan: "Off the Plane and Into Our Arms" 9/12/88

Tuchman, Barbara W.: "Tangling with Technology" (published as "Are We Smart Enough for Our Technology?") 10/29/84

Wasson, Glenn: "The Bee" (published as "The Strong and the Weak") 7/6/81

Weston, Eleanor: "Can I Keep It?" 6/13/88

Williams, Paul O.: "Potting and Poetry" (published as "A Poet Scanning Clay") 5/13/85; "Winter Meeting—a Christmas Sonnet" (sonnet) 12/18/84

Winder, David: "Snow" (published as "Meeting on the Same Ground") 10/18/77

Wolff, Theodore: "Face to Face" 12/4/86

Yamauchi, Wakako: "Wasteland Years" (published as "Surviving Wasteland Years") 11/8/88

Yemma, John: "The Commodore Was Home" 3/4/87